Dad's Book

Written by

Tom Sanderson

completed by his daughter Jan

Grosvenor House
Publishing Limited

This book is published by
Grosvenor House Publishing Ltd
Link House
140 The Broadway, Tolworth, Surrey, KT6 7HT.
www.grosvenorhousepublishing.co.uk

A CIP record for this book
is available from the British Library

ISBN 978-1-80381-911-2

Cover photo by Bernard G Mills
Email: bgmfoto2@ntlworld.com

Dedication

For Alice and Cathy, his granddaughters and Harry, Hetty and Tommy, the future.

My Eulogy

Well here we are, the day I've been dreading all my life, but now that day's arrived, I can see it's not the end of the story, it's just the day we move on to the next chapter.

Everyone here would agree what a shining light my father was, such a good, kind, talented, funny, unassuming perfect gentleman. Everyone has stories of his thoughtfulness, his quiet generosity, his wisdom and his sense of humour.

My earliest memories are of him coming home from work in winter, I'd be in bed and he'd come straight up to tuck me in, his ears would be freezing cold and he'd tell me stories about Africa. I remember him getting his silver trumpet out of its crocodile case and knocking out a few bars of 'Solitude'.

I remember going shopping at Affleck and Brown in Manchester, Mum would go off up the escalator to look for clothes and I would end up in the basement with him looking for nuts and bolts for some project he'd have on. I was his apprentice, he made sure I knew how to use a saw and change a plug, stuff every girl needs to know.

I never had brothers or sisters so he was always my best pal. I'd drag him into the sea all the time on holiday in Llangrannog, he was such good fun. One time we went in when it was really too rough, my mother was horrified but you always felt totally safe with him. He would make racing cars in the sand with loads of seats so that all the kids could sit one behind the other.

He was the person that everyone came to if they had a problem, knowing that whether it was a flat tyre or an affair of the heart, or anything in between, he would have the solution and he always did. He wouldn't necessarily tell you what it was but he'd help you work it out for yourself.

He wasn't afraid to confront a difficult situation but he did so with fairness, honesty and compassion. I can remember him telling me when I was quite small that there are two sides to every argument.

He was calm and rational. I never saw him lose his temper but a story he told me typifies what a gent he was. Apparently one night when there'd been a fatal accident on the A59 in Lancashire and he'd been shouting over the radio to send back up, using a bit of colourful language, he found out that one of the female radio operators had overheard the whole thing. The next day he went out and bought her chocolates to apologise!

He might have been 93 but he was young at heart. He used to say that he saw things through the same eyes even though his body was getting old. He was still playing golf at 90, he took up the banjo at 91, at 92 he learnt how to knit and he took great delight in telling the respiratory doctors at Eastbourne Hospital that yes ... he might have had asbestos in his garage in the '60's but he was still playing the trumpet 3 weeks ago!

Since he was a boy, motorbikes, cars and driving have been his passion. We went up to Scotland the year before he died to visit the ancestors' graves. On the way back he decided we'd go cross country on the famous A708 from Selkirk to the top of the motorway at Moffat. I'd spent the whole trip driving his big BMW like I had a basket of eggs in the car, we got to the first cattle grid and he said, "Move over..." talk about white knuckle ride, he went like the clappers. He mentioned it the week before he died, he was glad he got the chance for one last burn up.

Cath, my lovely mother, of course was the light of his life. They adored each other. They did everything together and latterly, when she developed Alzheimer's, he looked after her like a Saint. He was kindness and patience personified.

He never complained. He was always happy with his lot.

One night when I was staying with him before he went into hospital, he was really poorly, very weak and breathless. He was in bed and I could hear him mumbling. I thought he was having a bad dream so I went in to see if he was OK. He was singing! "Heaven ... I'm in Heaven ... and my heart beats so that I can hardly speak and I seem to find the happiness I seek ... when we're out together dancing cheek to cheek."

So that's how I'll be thinking of him, spinning round the dance floor in Heaven, dancing cheek to cheek with my Mum ... and all is well with the world.

His Death

Since my Mother had died, Dad had stopped playing golf. I used to go over 3 times a week to keep him company. We taught ourselves how to play the banjo ... not very well but enough to have some fun.

One day he confessed he was struggling with the hoovering so I said, "Do you want me to come to stay for a bit" and he said, "I'm tempted to say yes." So that was it, I moved in with him.

We had several trips to the doc's but they couldn't identify anything specific, until one morning, when we were supposed to go to see a specialist in geriatric care in Eastbourne, he was too weak to get out of bed. I rang to cancel the appointment and got short shrift from the locum doctor who sent an ambulance to take him off to hospital. We collected his kit together, he looked round his bedroom and said, "Right that's it then." I don't know if he knew he wouldn't see it again but I think he did. However, he went off in the ambulance telling them he needed to be back for his granddaughter's wedding in May.

He was in hospital for a week before we said our goodbyes and he passed away peacefully. The nurse asked if he was in any pain, he said "None whatsoever." She asked him how was his breathing, he said, "I can't breathe at all" and off he went to be with his beloved Cath.

This is his story

THOMAS SANDERSON ESQ.
of North Way, Seaford. East Sussex.
Monday 29-3-04. 10.25pm.

Chapter 1

Blackpool

This is to be the start of the autobiography of one Thomas Sanderson who was born on the 23rd of August 1920 at Spring Gardens, Common Edge Lane, Marton, Blackpool, Lancashire, the second of four children born to Alice Kate Sanderson (nee Beesley) known as 'Kit' and Douglas Sanderson, a serving Police Officer in the Lancashire Constabulary stationed at Lytham St Annes.

My elder brother George Alexander, born 4th November 1917 in Victoria Road, Aldershot, Hampshire, preceded me. I was followed by my sister Joan Alice born 13th May 1924 and younger brother, Douglas Elliot born 11th February 1927, both at Spring Gardens. We three being brought into this world by one Doctor Elliot who evidently did an excellent job as we all survived well into our 70's and 80's and was remembered by including his name when christening Douglas.

Our mother was a Southerner and I have scant knowledge of her background. She met my father when he was serving in the First World War when he was stationed at Borden Barracks, Hampshire. She lived in Grosvenor Road, Aldershot, with her mother and stepfather George Beesley, a really nice, quiet grandfather who drove a

Alice Kate Beesley

3

bus for the Aldershot and District Traction Company. Mum had a sister Maud, who was also married to a police officer in Guildford. My mother thought that she was her half sister until Maud died, when her birth certificate was found. Although it was never mentioned in the family, I believe that they were both illegitimate daughters of some wealthy family in whose service my grandmother was employed. My mother was quite well educated, although I never heard where she went to school. After being a housemaid at Busbridge Hall in Godalming she became travelling companion to Lady Kilmorey who had a property in Ireland at Mourne Park, Kilkeel, as well as a property on Park Lane in London. One of my mother's duties was to organise the servants and the luggage when they travelled to Ireland. When they returned to London for the 'season' she would have to go to Buckingham Palace in the pony and trap to inform the the Palace of their return so that the family would receive invites to social gatherings. I believe they spent some time in Ireland during the rise of Sin Fein. She had already met, and fallen in love with her first fiancé, John (known as Jack) Phillips of Godalming, who later became the first radio officer for Marconi on the fated Titanic. They were engaged at the time of Jack's death. The engagement ring, which was given to my grandmother for safe keeping, was subsequently given to my sister Joan who, after having it remodelled, lost it, whilst trailing her hand it the waters of Lake Windermere from a rowing boat.

After Jack's death and whilst in Ireland, Mother was leaving church one Sunday morning, with the Kilmoreys when they were stoned by a crowd of Catholics. As a result, she was sent home to recuperate and it was during this time that she met my father. I believe they were married within six months. That would be Christmas Day 1916. I do not know at which church the ceremony took place.

Douglas and Kit's wedding 25.12.1916

My father's family consisted of an elder brother, Alexander, who was killed at Gallipoli in the First World War, sisters Emily, Elsie, Matilda and Ida. My grandmother, Emily Louise, nee Davidson born 7.6.1861, in later life lived with Matilda (known as Aunty Till) in a terraced house in Eccles, Lancashire.

My paternal grandfather, Thomas Sanderson, died after returning from South Africa where he served in the Medical Corps during the Boer War. In civilian life he had been a wire weaver in Manchester. He was of Scottish origin born in Glasgow 13.3.1865. Grandma's parents were

Father's family with Mum and George

Tom Davidson and Matilda Hobson from the Rochester area, Kent.

We have a book, 'Tom Brown's School Days' which is in poor condition and possibly a first edition. It is inscribed in the flyleaf, 'Alexander Sanderson Worsley Road, Winton.' This was the Alexander who died at Gallipoli. Inside this

Birthday Telegram

6

book we have recently found a telegram from my father addressed to my mother at 98 Grosvenor Road, Aldershot, wishing her many happy returns of her birthday, dated 9th January 1918.

Our house, as far as I remember, was a two up two down in a terrace of about four or six. There was no bathroom and the toilet was built of brick in the back yard. It consisted of a scrubbed wooden board with a hole in it underneath which was a metal bucket. The outer wall of the toilet was part of the back wall of the yard and there was a wooden back yard gate. Access to the bucket could be obtained via a wooden door in the outside wall. Once a week a character known as Joe Whitehead, known to us as 'Nitty Whiskers' as he had a white beard, came around the back of the row emptying the 'privies' as they were known. His vehicle was horse drawn and consisted of a large metal tank, slung crossways between the two wheels of the cart.

There was no electricity or gas. Lighting was by means of candles or paraffin lamps. Going to the toilet in the evenings involved lighting a candle and shielding it from the wind as one went down the yard. (Light was necessary to look for spiders!)

The living room fireplace had an oven along side and a damper to draw out which caused the draught to circulate the heat around the oven. This was used to do all the cooking, cakes, bread etc. Trivets on either side were used for boiling the kettle, frying etc. I have fond memories of arriving home from school to a roaring fire with my mother toasting crumpets with a long toasting fork in front of the fire. The crumpets were purchased from a man who hawked them around the district, selling them from a large wickerwork basket with a white cloth over it. Scrumptious!

A new invention called the 'wireless' was developing about the time of my early childhood. I think I would be about two when the BBC came into being. Screwing down three knobs, which were in front of three valves, operated our first radio. As they were screwed down, the valves started to glow and sound came through the headphones. After some time we obtained a speaker and we were all able to listen at the same time. Two batteries, one a dry cell type and the other a wet, chargeable type powered this. My father made a crystal set, which was screwed to a board measuring about a foot long by six to eight inches deep. This worked without valves as they were substituted by what was known as a 'cat's whisker'. Reception was quite weak but he was able to take it to Aintree, when on duty at the Grand National and follow the commentary of the race as it took place through a set of headphones. I reckon that must have been one of the first portable radios.

George and Tom aged 2

Our small front garden was separated from next-door by a small wall capped with pointed capping tiles which I was able to roll over whenever I could smell cooking from our neighbour's kitchen when I was usually given the bowl to clean out. Mrs Singleton was her name. She had a husband Ralf and a daughter (I think adopted)(who's name I cannot remember at the moment) who was later to be the subject of sexual abuse by her stepfather who was arrested by my father and subsequently received a custodial sentence. I can remember being in their house at mealtimes and the girl, who was then about ten or eleven was not allowed to sit at the table but had to stand to eat her meals. I felt very sorry for that girl even though I would be only four or five years old. Next-door to them or next door but one lived a family called Melling. They had a son called Falshaw who was older than me but younger than George. He was 'famous'. He had an Aunt who worked in the film studios in London. I think she was a seamstress working on the costumes but to us, that was quite glamorous. I've never met another Falshaw since! There were no buildings on the opposite side of the road as the ground was used as a market garden. The house was either rented or owned by the police and as our family grew they became obliged to find us more suitable accommodation, which we will come to later.

On our side of the road and some hundred yards or so towards Blackpool, was a sweet factory where we used to look in at the open doors to watch them making Blackpool Rock. The rock was made in huge chunks, the words 'Blackpool Rock' inserted as large, black pieces of spun sugar, assembled in a certain order with the main silver pieces and the whole was covered with the red outer layer. The whole piece, which appeared very hot, was then rolled and pulled on hot steel tables, which were covered in powdered sugar. The smell and heat, which emanated from that doorway, will live with me for the rest of my days.

Another fifty yards or so and on the opposite side of the road was the local paper shop. The occupants, the Fitzgerald family were family friends and it was in David Fitzgerald's open topped Singer 9 that I had a ride in my first motorcar. It had electric headlights, which I thought were marvellous. The Fitzgeralds had two children, a daughter, whose name I can't remember and a son called Sonny. He had a pedal car and we loved to go down to his place for a ride. His mother made the best ice cream I've ever tasted. She kept it inside the shop in a large red container which had the metal ice cream container in the centre surrounded by ice. Sadly Sonny died when he was quite young. I don't think he reached school age.

George had started school rather late due to some illness which delayed his attendance but had been travelling to Waterloo Road School, Blackpool some 12 to 15 months before me, firstly by three-wheeled tricycle, then by a Hercules bicycle and the tricycle was passed on to me. The journey to school was about a mile and a half to two miles in distance and was an excellent start to develop the muscles and stamina of a growing five year old! Needless to say, I was unable to keep up with the Hercules and often got left behind.

One Christmas morning, that would be 1925 or 1926, I came down stairs to find a brand new Runwell cycle leaning against the settee. Life was to be much easier from then on but first I had to master the balancing bit. My father fitted blocks to the pedals and off we went down the road as fast as he could run!! From then on my trips to school required much less effort except when the wind blew. They do not call it Breezy Blackpool for nothing! One stretch of the journey had terraced houses on either side of the road and the wind would increase to gale force between these. There were times when it did reduce me to tears. Another lesson in perseverance! Meals at school were non-existent in those days although I seem to remember school milk in little bottles but that could have been much later. We did get Horlicks provided for a small fee at one school, I can't remember which but I can remember that it was made with water!

Lunch or dinner as we called it, consisted of sandwiches, prepared by our mother, which we ate whilst sitting on the hot water pipes in the cloakroom often among damp, smelly outdoor clothing.

My earliest recollections are of summer weather, playing in the roadway running after the horse buses, which used our road as part of a circular tour around Blackpool.

The passengers sat up on raised seats, one either side with a passage down the centre and three steps at the back. It was drawn by a pair of horses and we kids would climb on the steps and hitch a ride without the knowledge of the driver (most often) and go a couple of hundred yards down the road and wait for the bus going in the opposite direction. Hot summers meant sticky tar on the road, which was very useful for weighting the tips of our arrows which we fired from bows made from the ribs of old umbrellas bound with string and were powerful enough to fire an arrow clear over the house.

Towards St Annes from our house was a pub called The Shovels. There is still one there by that name but I'm not sure that it is on the same site. Across from The Shovels was the road to Squires Gate and just around the corner of this road was a blacksmith's shop. It was called a blacksmith's shop although it was just a forge with bellows operated by a long handle where the blacksmith's striker would pump it up and down and create a terrific amount of heat to get the steel for whatever they were making, almost white hot. They would then take it out of the furnace with long tongs and beat it into shape on the anvil. They were always making horseshoes and shoeing the horses in the doorway. They wore thick leather aprons and would get the horse's hoof between their legs and fit the shoe by applying it to the hoof while it was still very hot. It would sizzle, create a lot of smoke and a smell that lives forever in one's mind. We used to get a go at operating the bellows if there were no horses about. I say operating, we were helping to operate, as it was much too heavy for us to pull down on our own. These blacksmiths were highly skilled craftsmen. I can still remember watching him weld two pieces of steel with the heat of the forge and his hammer. All these experiences must have had a bearing on my future outlook on life in general and my appreciation of engineers and engineering.

There were many trips by the family into Blackpool with picnics on the sands, which appeared very clean then although there were a number of large pipes, covered in concrete, taking something out to sea. I now realise what those pipes contained! Also the pleasure beach was another favourite for some people. I'm afraid I was not one of them as anything that turns around turns my stomach around and I kept well away and continue to do so. There was a big wheel there but it had to be removed for some reason (I think storm damage) and it changed the whole appearance of the Golden Mile i.e. from the Pleasure Beach to the Tower where all the 'kiss me quick' shops, Madam Tussauds, candy floss, bearded lady, fortune tellers etc had their shops. It was nothing like the size of the London Eye but we thought it was pretty big though. It was known as 'The Big Wheel'. I never went on it.

Blackpool was the centre of the northern wakes weeks. The one week a year when the cotton towns took it in turn to close for a week while the workers took a week's holiday. The inhabitants of these towns would take off for a week. The shops would close and the town would become 'dead'. The great majority going off to Blackpool where, for 7 days they would really let their hair down and live it up for a few days as their normal everyday lives were pretty hard. The weavers, (mainly women) would start in the weaving shed at 6am when the looms would start up and they would be there until 6pm. One weaver would look after several looms and the noise created by the machinery was deafening. Consequently, they all learned to lip read, which came in very handy in their social life! Women did not go into pubs in those days or smoke in public. Only 'loose' women were to be found in bars. Things changed after 3rd Sept. 1939. Blackpool pre war, consisted mainly of hotels and boarding houses and could accommodate many thousands of people. This came in very handy when the 2nd World War broke out, as I was to return to one of those boarding houses!

Blackpool had its illuminations from as far back as I remember. The purpose being to try and extend the holiday season. Special trams would be decorated. 'The Gondola' was one, then there was 'Progress'. A visit to the 'lights' was not considered complete unless we saw at least one of them. Trams would traverse the streets in those days. They only travel the length of the prom now from Fleetwood to Squires Gate. The famous tower, when I was young, was famous for its zoo underground. There were lions and tigers and many other animals pacing up and down and going round and round in sawdust covered cages. There were certain feeding times published when the animals would be thrown chunks of meat to devour. It was cruel but at the time we didn't realise how cruel, as that was the way things were at zoos.

About this time my father had a black Airedale type dog, it was his constant companion and would often accompany him when on night duty. On one occasion when the dog was left at home in the front room, it decided my father was not going out without it, so it jumped through the front window to get out. Strangely enough, it was not injured but the window was in a mess.

Once a year, we would visit our grandparents in Aldershot. Sometimes we would travel to London by train, cross from Euston Station to Victoria by taxi to catch the train to Aldershot. On other occasions we would make the journey by road in a Seagull or John Bull coach as far as London. This was quite an adventure for us kids especially when we stopped off at Gamages or Selfridges to visit their toy department. On one occasion my brother George was bought an air rifle and I had a bow and arrows. These we carried on the open top of a London bus on our journey across the capital. I was wearing an eye patch as I had injured my left eye by falling on a stick. Other passengers made many remarks. I had trouble with sticks! I also injured the roof of my mouth with a stick. How, I cannot remember! Probably falling with it in my mouth. All injuries evidently healed satisfactorily as I lived to tell the tale and the scars are barely noticeable.

Aldershot was and still is a garrison town but in the nineteen thirties there were barracks galore. A great treat for us was to go to the church parades on a Sunday morning, when all the regiments would parade in full dress with banners flying and bands playing as they marched up the avenue to the church at the top. There were drum and fife bands of the Irish regiments, Scottish pipe bands with their kilts, white spats, bear skins etc. The Guards regiments all with their own bands. Quite a magnificent sight I thought. Even the mounted regiments turned out. I don't know where they all went when they all got to the top of the avenue as they all certainly couldn't get into the church.

Some of the cavalry regiments would allow the public to walk through and look at the horses in the stables. They were all spotless. Each horse had its own stall with its name and all the rosettes that it had won at various events. Show jumping, tent pegging etc. At times when the public were not allowed in, the entrance to the stables, which was along side the footpath at one particular barracks, was roped off with thick blancoed rope, the ends of which were inserted into polished brass sockets which were then hooked across the entrance. (Blanco was a white paste much used in the services to whiten fabrics such as webbing and rope.) The reason for the above preamble is that on one occasion when passing this stable with my mother and father, and the rope was across the entrance, I decided to sit on the rope and have a swing. One end of the rope came out of its socket, I sat on the floor and made a hasty retreat from the area before anyone found out. I crossed the road years after, when passing those stables in case anyone recognised me.

Another place George and I enjoyed visiting when in Aldershot was Farnborough Aerodrome. Father used to take us walking over the common which was on the opposite side of the flying field to the buildings. It was an experimental establishment owned I believe by the

Government. I remember seeing the first autogiro flying there as well as a few early experimental bombers.

We had many trips to Blackpool from our house in Marton Moss (as this part of the district was known), as there were no food shops in the local vicinity. I remember going with my brother George to the 'Home and Colonial' grocers in Blackpool for bacon and it had to be "the bit with the two little bones in" as my mother would say. We were fascinated by the way the grocer would serve butter by cutting it from a large block and patting it with two wooden paddles into the shape that he wanted, before finally packing it in greaseproof paper. Butter had to be New Zealand as Mother believed in supporting the Empire as it was then. Shopping could not be completed without a visit to the model shop where a Hornby train set was laid out in the window and if we were lucky it would be running. It was quite a complicated layout as it disappeared out of the window at times and there were many different engines and coaches in the system. Fascinating for young boys in those days!! They sometimes had a small steam engine working, driving a windmill. I can't remember much about the shop or its name but I know where it is or was!

Tom, Joan and George September 1924

As two of my siblings and I were born at this house it is sad that it no longer exists. I have no recollection of my sister's birth but I can clearly remember Doctor Elliott arriving at the front door to deliver brother Douglas. My father went to the door. It was a double door as there was a front door and a vestibule door. As my father got to the front door, my sister Joan was in close attendance and clinging on to his leg. I was not far behind and was given the job of looking after Joan as she was getting quite excited and demanding to know why she could not follow Dad and the doctor upstairs. On being told later that we had a baby brother she wanted to know where it had come from and was satisfied with the explanation that the doctor had brought it in that black bag.

Not long after Doug was born, we were moved to a Police House at Peel crossroads which was right on the A583, the main road from Preston to Blackpool. As travellers passed our garden, the road took a bend to the right and went up hill and they got their first glimpse of Blackpool Tower which was just over 3 miles away as was Waterloo Road School. For quite some time George and

The family on the Isle of Wight Ferry

I travelled to Waterloo Road on our cycles. Many times we had to walk home especially if the weather was bad or we had a puncture and our kindly Belfast Tea company driver had called for us in his Morris van on his way to Blackpool in the morning. Eventually, Mother decided that it was too much for me and I was enrolled at Little Marton School, which was only about a mile away.

Little Marton School consisted of a Headmaster and a teacher and the school was divided between them. I struggled at first as at my old school I was still printing and my age group at Little Marton were doing proper writing. One can imagine the mess that my early efforts were in! However, I did eventually manage a passable script and have always blamed my clumsy or untidy writing on having to change schools.

Peel was a house well into the countryside. We had neighbours as the house was a semi-detached but I cannot remember much about them. I think he was a teacher employed by the local education authority, as our house was a Police Station. There was no office as such, but they evidently owned the place as they just stuck up a plate, which displayed 'Police Station' so that anyone could come knocking at the door, day or night.

I suppose I would have been 7 or 8 at Peel. Most of the summer holidays, George and I would spend hours, sitting on our fence along side the main road, with jugs of water and glasses to quench the thirst of passing cyclists. We could have made a fortune but we never charged. At this time I knew every vehicle that passed, makes that have all gone into oblivion years ago. Royal Ruby, Clino, Rex Acme, AJS, Panther, Scott, Standard, BSA, Norton etc. etc. One or two names are still around but none are actually designed and made here. Foreign companies have bought out most and the others buy in bits and screw them together. Woe is me! Where are the Brunels of today?

At this house, we became dog breeders and pigeon fanciers. Father had an Alsation bitch which we called Rinty after Rin Tin Tin which was a famous dog of the silent cinema days. Rinty was very protective of we kids. My father was once warned about poachers down the woods, which turned out to be George and myself out with our airguns and Rinty looking for rabbits. I don't ever remember finding any. We were both taught to shoot by Dad. (This got me into a bit of trouble when we lived in Lancaster but I digress!) On another occasion our sister Joan went missing one evening. The 'hue and cry' was put into operation and after much searching she was found in the kennel with Rinty and her litter of pups. That dog became very protective of Joan. The local Sergeant, when paying my father a visit once went to pick Joan up in a friendly sort of way when Rinty saw him! Father had a lot of explaining and apologising to do. I don't think the Sergeant was actually bitten but he never came through the front gate again.

We had some lovely fan tailed pigeons at Peel. Before they came, a loft was constructed on the top of a long pole and the pigeons duly arrived. I believe they are supposed to be confined in their new home for some time before letting them out. We evidently did not confine them long enough as when they were released they made a nice circle and flew off home. More appeared but I don't know if they were the originals. We did manage to breed these Fan Tails. However, my interest in pigeons ceased after Mother served up a lovely (to some people) pigeon pie. I refused it and suffered the consequences. Bed on an empty stomach.

It was at Peel that we, the children, became the victims of a dreaded virus known as Scarlet Fever. It was quite a serious condition in those days and involved isolation. First, George went down with it and went off to the Isolation Hospital at Moss Side. When he returned, I caught it and was taken off to the hospital where we were kept in isolation for about 4 or 5 weeks. My recollections of this hospital are quite clear. I can still see the large ward with its

Family portrait

highly polished brown lino floor. There was a large coke stove, mounted on an oval concrete plinth in the middle. This was surrounded by an oval, wire fireguard, which had a polished brass rail around the top. Each morning the brass rail would be polished, as would the lino floor. My main recollection of this ward is one of cleanliness and polish. This stove was the only method of heating the ward and I was there over Christmas. When my parents came to visit, they had to stand on a wooden platform outside the building and look in at us through the window. They must have been frozen. The ward was decorated for Christmas but the only food that I can remember is watery rice pudding and jam butties. Oh yes! A nurse came round after our meal and gave us a sweet. I was also suffering a large cold sore on the corner of my mouth and the same nurse would come round once a day with a kidney bowl, a pair of tweezers and some smelly liquid and pick the scab off then dab this smelly liquid on. It was agony! I have smelled that smell since. It is the smell that comes from the liquid they use for treating head lice.

The story went around the inmates that we would be kept in isolation until our feet started to peel. I use to scrutinise mine every day and yes, they did start to peel but they had just about finished by the time I got out. One of the ways that we passed some of the time was fighting with rolled up newspaper. We would roll up a broadsheet as tight as possible and it would become quite hard. The tighter the roll the harder it became and the longer it would last when defending one's bed space. Having spent Christmas in isolation my presents were there for me when I arrived home. One that I remember was a boxer made of dark chocolate. It must have been nearly a foot tall.

Well, not long after my return home, Douglas caught it. As soon as the doctor diagnosed it Joan decided that Doug was not going to hospital without her so she promptly gave him a cuddle, caught it herself, and the pair of them went off to isolation together.

Across the road from us was a small garage that didn't seem to be open very often. There were two old cars parked at the back that we used to play in. I remember one was an American Buick. It wouldn't go but we used to imagine travelling the world in it.

It was at Peel that I had my first ride on the pillion of a motorcycle. I think it belonged to a distant relative although I can't remember ever meeting him since. It was a B.S.A, twin cylinder, combination. The sidecar was a bit boat shaped and the whole outfit seemed rather large but the acceleration was fantastic. I had never experienced anything like it before and I think the motorcycle bug bit at that very moment, as it has always been my favourite mode of transport.

Chapter 2

Farnworth/Kearsley

Before moving on to our next abode I should include a little about Little Marton School. The building still exists although it is no longer a school. I visited the area a few years ago and took a photograph of it.

Little Marton School years later

Nothing appears to have changed. The front yard and the low wall are still there. We used to play rounders in the front yard. The school would divide into two teams and fielders would be placed across the road in the field along side. The best hits would end up in the field. Traffic on this road was very light in those days and I don't think anyone was ever involved in an accident. As I referred to before, there were only two teaching staff, which consisted of a headmaster and a lady teacher. Their names escape me for the moment.

Class photo - yours truly 3rd row back centre

The head was responsible for the discipline of the school. Those in need of his services, when sent to him, would be given his penknife to go into the wood next to the school and cut himself a cane. The problem was, whether to cut a thin or a thick one. I can't remember ever having the problem myself.

Peel was the first introduction of the family to First Aid. A circular bus would pass our door on one of its excursions from Blackpool. On one occasion, the driver must have thought that his engine was overheating. He stopped outside our gate, suspecting that the radiator was short of water, he decided to have a look. On removing the radiator cap, the pressure of steam shot up into his face. Fortunately, my mother was at home and promptly treated his face with a bicarbonate of soda solution. This was successful in preventing his face from blistering badly. He was sent off to hospital and Mother eventually received a letter of thanks from the bus company. I cannot remember any reward but it has been a good lesson for the four of us over the years whenever a scald or burn has occurred in our families. A policeman's wife often became an unpaid assistant and it was more or less expected of her.

It was from Peel that Dad took us to our first motor cycle dirt track racing at Squires Gate track. Wilf McCluer was the star rider as I remember. He was riding a Scott or a Douglas as these seemed to be the popular dirt track bike of the period. George and I got quite keen and went whenever they had a meeting during the short while that we were there. Squires Gate also had and still has, the airport for Blackpool. There were flights around the tower for about five shillings, which was far too expensive for us, but it was fascinating for us to watch the take offs and landings. I was to visit Squires Gate Airport again in 1940.

My gift of The Golden Budget for Boys

Around 1928, The Lancashire Constabulary, in its wisdom, decided that my father would be transferred to a house in Trafford Street, Farnworth. This was quite a change for us as Farnworth was a much more industrial area situated alongside Bolton. Industries were mainly cotton, coal mining and heavy engineering.

It was here that I realised that I could read as we had a library virtually at the end of the street. My interest then was the American mail delivery service, which existed before the telegraph came into being. It was known as The Pony Express. I must have read every book in the library on the subject. In my imagination, I rode with them across America, changing horses every few miles. They did not carry guns as they would only add to the weight,

Frontispiece of the Golden Budget ...
looks like George copped it this time

and speed was the essential factor as they out-paced the Indians by their superior horses and riding skills. All exciting reading for an 8/9 year old.

George, who had remained at Waterloo Road School, was showing some academic promise as he had passed the 11+ and got a scholarship to Farnworth Grammar School. I was enrolled at Queen Street School as was my sister Joan, who had reached school age. Queen Street does not have very pleasant memories for me! Being a stranger to some people gives them an excuse to bully and I'm afraid I was the victim of a certain clique who decided that I was to be their target. However, I lived to tell the tale and have not suffered unduly although, maybe, that is for others to decide!

The kitting out of George for his new school was a major event in our household. Special clothes for PT, special clothes for rugby, blazer with badge etc, etc. and even proper boots for playing rugby! Money was not very plentiful in those days as it was the beginning of the slump of the 1930's and many men were out of work. A policeman's wage was considered quite good and it was regular!

Farnworth was a town, which, among other things, had cinemas. This was the time of silent films, when a pianist accompanied the action. The old lady that I remember would sit at her piano to the right of and just in the front of the screen. She would follow the action with the correct tempo of music, speeding up when the action speeded up and going into a lullaby for the dreamy sequences. It seemed to work very well. We were watching the great cowboy actors of the silents. Tom Mix and his horse Tony who were always the heroes. Great comics such as Charlie Chaplin, Buster Keaton to name a couple. George and I would go along to the matinee on a Saturday afternoon. I think we paid 1 penny to get in and we were also given a penny for a bar of nougat. It was all active picture going. The audience got involved with booing the villain and cheering the hero. The acting was all very exaggerated and I blame that lady on the piano for creating a lot of our mental instability! Another of my problems at this time was my inability to read the captions fast enough and George would get really annoyed with me asking, "What did it say?" The excitement would also create the urge for me to go to the toilet and, not wishing to miss any of the action, I would sometimes wait too long and have to make a mad dash to the back to the toilet! It was at this cinema that I saw my first 'talky'. It was Al Jolson in 'The Singing Fool'. Now that was really something! We continued going to the silent films for some time before the lady at the piano became redundant.

We did not stay long in Farnworth, probably about 12 months, when Father was promoted to sergeant and we were moved to Kearsley, which was a few miles down the main road towards Manchester. Here we were to occupy the Police Station at Kearsley, which had Kearsley St Stephens School practically outside the back yard gate. The move from Farnworth was carried out with a large van pulled by a pair of shire horses. The police force had their own furniture removal vans but I think a private contractor did this, as it was such a short move. I was allowed to travel with the driver and I remember him letting me have hold of the reins as the horses trotted along. I don't know what would have happened if I had pulled them.

I have fond memories of Kearsley! I would be about 10 or 11 and noticing that there were girls at our school. Alice Watson became my first love but she never knew about it. She was clever! She could tuck her skirt into her knickers and stand on her hands!! Brilliant! Unfortunately for me, someone had designs on me! She wasn't the prettiest girl in the class. The name escapes me!

Kearsley St Stephens had a prize brass band and I joined the junior section and was given instruction in playing the cornet. The first tune we learned was 'Jesus Shall Reign Where'er the Sun' to the tune of Rimmington I believe. I was given a smart uniform and cap and joined the band as one of the third cornets, which consisted mainly of the umpa, umpa, bits. We learned plenty of marches and learned to read music. The band was engaged to play for lots of 'walking day' processions, summer fetes etc. and at Christmas time we went around the local pubs playing carols. The collection was shared between us. Most of my practising was done alongside the hot water cistern in the bathroom, sitting on the toilet seat. It was the only room in the house apart from the living room that had any heat as this was in the days before central heating became the norm. The cosy, warm houses of today tend to make one forget the days before central heating. It was not uncommon to find ice in the bedroom, particularly on the windows and windowsill. Going to bed in the winter and getting in between ice-cold sheets is something to remember!!

The prize, senior band took part in the annual brass band competitions at Belle Vue, Manchester. All the bands would be given the same piece of music to rehearse and then appear at the venue on a certain date to perform. The judges were positioned in a cubicle where they could not see which band was playing and adjudicated on what they heard. Some say that there was a fiddle going on, as one band would perhaps give an extra half beat on a particular note to identify to a certain judge which band was playing. All the bandsmen were listening out for this as the whole thing was really competitive. We in the junior band had to practice the same piece in case someone went sick. There had to be an instant competent replacement. My most lasting memory of this competition was two, rather inebriated cornet players, playing 'The Stein Song' outside the bar, in two part harmony, without a wrong note. I thought it was amazing and I will never forget it. George later joined the band playing a tenor horn. Joan became a Brownie and Douglas started school in the infant's section at St Stephens. We had quite a turn out on Armistice Day parades with the 'Old Man' in charge!

Armistice Day Parade

The police station was formerly a pub. There was a central corridor, which had a polished marble surface, which sloped gradually towards the rear, when it dropped down one step. It was a perfect surface for roller-skating down. I once met a stranger roaming about at the back of our house looking for the toilets as he thought it was still a pub. At the front and to the right of the front door, was the Office. This had a high, mahogany desk and tall stools for the policemen to use when writing reports etc. As it was a sort of out station, it was not manned continuously and the telephone was of the stand up type with the earpiece hung on a cradle on it. To call up the main station one had to lift the receiver, turn a handle on a wooden box alongside, and wait for a reply. Father had great trouble with Douglas, who was about 5 years old at the time, not only answering the phone, but also ringing H.Q. at times. This became quite serious when he answered the phone on one occasion and the call turned out to be someone reporting an accident and no action was taken for some time. He was banned from the office after that. Mother, and we the elder boys were quite used to answering the police calls, as I believe Mother was expected to do if there was no one else about. She also had the care of lost children etc. etc. all without

29

pay! Cleaning of the police part of the premises was done by policemen on night duty or the early morning shift if it had been a busy night. Floors would be polished, including the corridor (as I was to find out many years later when I was told by a Detective Superintendent that he used to do that cleaning before I used it as a roller skating rink.) That is part of another story that may be included later.

Among the clutter, which accompanied our family from house to house, was a pair of spiked, leather running shoes. No one had ever laid claim to them and I remember they were green with mould. It would appear that they were a relic of my father's army days. Kearsley was a sub station of Bolton Division and the great day in their calendar was the annual sports day. Father decided to support the

Physical Training

Division and entered him, Joan and myself in the various age group 100-yard sprints. Out came the spikes and after much cleaning and rubbing with dubbin, they became half presentable. Joan and I were taken to the field at the back of the school and trained in the art of starting when the gun went off. This went on for all of 10 minutes when we got bored and pronounced ourselves ready for competition. The great day of the sports arrived and the family caught the bus into Bolton and duly presented we, the contestants, to the starter. I was given a 9-yard handicap. In Joan's heat she appeared about halfway down the track and I believe Dad was off scratch. However, results were a win for Father, a win for me and a third for Joan. We practically cleaned up. My father won a lovely gold watch for my mother, I won a gold watch for myself and I cannot remember what Joan won. Whatever happened to the spiked shoes I have no idea, as I never saw them again, nor did we take part in any more sports days. We were probably off to Lancaster before the next one came around.

I enjoyed St Stephen's School although we had some very strict members of staff. One used to carry the centre cane from an umbrella all the time. He used it on occasions! He also gave us a break between lessons when one of the pupils had to stand out in front of the class and tell a joke.

I sat the dreaded 11+ from this school and failed. It was called 'the scholarship' then and when one passed, there was a certain amount of money available to cover the costs. We, the entrants, had to travel to Farnworth to sit the examination. Complete with pens, pencil, ruler and rubber, about five of us from St Stephens, arrived at the examination room. We took our places as ordered and sat quietly at our desks until the papers were handed out. I looked at mine, read it through and tears came into my eyes. There were about two questions that I could attempt to answer. The rest were a complete mystery. There was nothing resembling anything that I had ever been taught. The following papers were just as bad and I knew that I would never pass before I left the room.

On returning to our school, the staff asked for our examination questions and we were unable to supply them, as we were required to write our answers on the same papers as the questions were on and of course, these were handed in. I do not remember anyone passing that year. I was very disappointed and felt terrible about it as I felt that I had let my parents down. I have never before expressed my feelings about this examination but I really believe that few of us were meant to pass that examination that year and I am convinced it was all about money and the grants that would have to be paid out. The whole country was in the grip of a financial depression. Many people were unemployed and workers were marching to London to lobby the government about doing something to help but I'm afraid that it did little good. My mother offered to pay for me to go to the Grammar School with George, but I felt too settled where I was and I was allowed to stay. Alas, the Constabulary had other ideas!

Not a lot happened that I remember apart from getting knocked off my father's bicycle by a car when nipping down to Farnworth one dinnertime. I was not injured apart from a few cuts and bruises. Father was not very pleased!

Chapter 3

Lancaster

Somewhere about my 12th birthday, the pictures were down again and we were off to Lancaster as my father had been moved to occupy a post of instructor in the Lancashire Constabulary Training School that was situated in Lancaster Castle. I had, reluctantly, to return my cornet and uniform and once again suffer the trauma of changing schools.

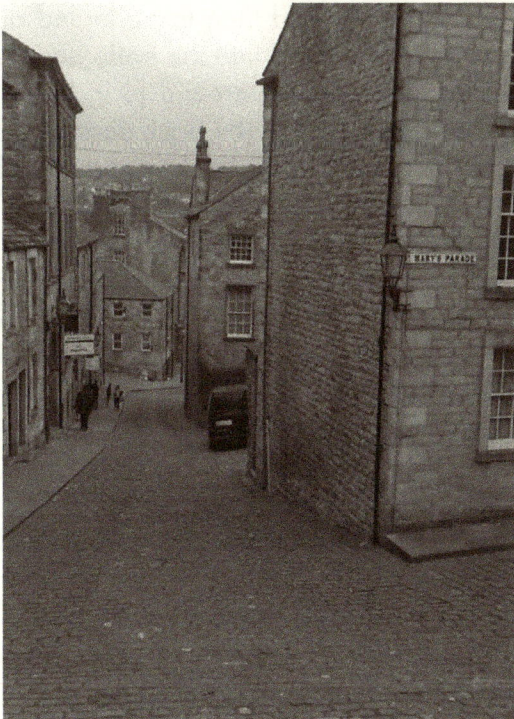

St Mary's Parade/Nippy (Nip) Hill

At Lancaster, we occupied a house in a terrace known as St Mary's Parade. This was just below the Castle wall in the direction of St Mary's Church. The terrace was built on a steep hill. The house had three stories at the front and four at the back. The lower floor was really a cellar and contained a bath with a solid lid over it, which could be raised when one wanted to use the bath. It was, of course, necessary to remove Joan's white mice first as this lid became a handy bench for all sorts of things! This operation was not to be taken lightly, as it needed careful organisation. Across from the bath was a brick boiler with a large copper cauldron sunk into the middle of it. When one wanted hot water, the cauldron would be filled and a fire set in the grate below. The length of time taken to heat the water would depend on the fuel available and the amount of stoking that one did. The hot water had then to be ladled out, carried across the room and poured into the bath. It was a nice big bath to enjoy when one got around to it, but it was a bit draughty when one got out!! The back door was along side the bath and this led out to the back yard that had our brick toilet (water closet) in it, as did the house next door. Heating in these houses was by means of a coal fire in the lounge or living room. The coal had to be stored somewhere and ours, at this house was stored in the front of the cellar. There was a manhole in the pavement outside our front window, covered with a cast iron cover. When coal was delivered, it would be emptied from the sacks into the hole, eventually piling up in our cellar. We then had to carry it upstairs to the fireplace.

A sort of communal yard ran along the back of the terrace. Each house had its own toilet situated at the rear. Access to the rear of the houses further along the terrace was through our yard then up four or five stone steps, with an iron railing alongside. These became the stage for sister Joan, who was taking ballet lessons at the time, to perform for all and sundry that happened to be around. The exit from this yard was through a wooden gate into a little cobbled ginnel or twitten, known as Nippy Hill. This led down to a rather grand house, situated at the back of our terrace. It was known as The Judges' Lodgings as it was used to house the Assize Court Judge when the court was sitting. The Assize Court was situated at the rear of the Castle and there would be much pomp and ceremony when he paraded to the Court in his full regalia. Full Police escort was provided, with recruits from the training school, dressed in best uniform with white gloves, and Father in charge. (Ex Company Sergeant Major with the 5th Manchester Regiment.)

Because of the steepness of Nippy Hill, my bedroom window was roughly at the level of the chimney pots of The Judges' Lodgings. The devil finding work for idle fingers, especially when crooked around the trigger of an air rifle, caused some consternation when injured crows and starlings began turning up at the rear of the Judges' abode. George and I were in competition as to who could hit the most! Someone made diligent enquiries, but it was many years later that I heard about it! However, my respect for all animals has developed as my age has increased and I would be appalled at that sort of behaviour today.

The Castle became one of our best playgrounds in Lancaster. The Superintendent in charge, whose family lived in part of the Castle, one by the name of Philpot, had two sons and we often spent days in the Castle grounds, exploring the dungeons, witches' tower, gallows etc. The rear of the Castle was open to visitors who were conducted around the dungeons, Norman Keep, Shire Hall, Assize Court, Torture Chamber etc. I was locked in the dungeon with Justine once, years later, when we paid a visit to the visitors section of the Castle. The front part, which was the training school, and was the former prison, was closed to the public. This part contained the central lawn with its small cannon and pyramid of cannon balls. These were approximately 8 inches in diameter and were kept in shining order by being black-leaded by the duty student.

The pyramid of cannon balls, I should think about twelve to fourteen in all, were piled at the front point of the triangular lawn with the cannon immediately behind. From the front point of the lawn, the flagstones sloped steeply down to the inner iron gates situated about a vehicle's length from the double oak front doors of the castle, between which the portcullis was secured in the up position and had been for so many years that I doubt it would ever move again. The iron gates were always kept open since the prison days. Entrance to the front doors was gained by ringing the bell and the duty officer would leave his office and unlock the small door to allow pedestrians in or swing open the double doors for vehicle entry. The weight of these doors was taken, not only by the hinges but also by wheels mounted on the bottom, leading edges. These ran on curved iron inserts in the flags, which no doubt helped to lighten the load when swinging them open.

There were occasions when a cannon ball was dislodged from the pile at the corner of the lawn and the whole lot would be set in motion towards the front doors with the resultant, bang, bang, bang as they collided with it, bringing the duty officer flying out of his 'slumbers' to detect the cause! There was never anyone about, as the place was a warren of hiding places. (I never succeeded in convincing my father that expansion and contraction may have dislodged those cannonballs!)

Alongside the front inner wall, near the Witches' Well, was a large rectangular grid, which was pretty overgrown with grass, and one could not see underneath it, as it appeared to be solid. It was rumoured that there was, at one time, a tunnel, which led from the Castle to the banks of the River Lune, and we believed that it was under this grid, although it has never been confirmed to my knowledge.

The Witches' Well was a small dungeon where the famous Lancashire Witches were imprisoned. It consisted of an entrance door, where after passing through, on one's immediate left, was a wall about four feet high, behind which was a well. It was quite deep as two or three seconds would elapse before the splash after throwing a stone down. Proceeding past the well, down a steep flight of nine or ten stone steps, one came to a dungeon about twelve feet in diameter. This was in complete darkness. The stone walls had deep holes dug into the sides, which we were told had been done by the witches trying to claw their way out. It seemed quite feasible when considering how dark, damp and overcrowded it must have been.

There was a gymnasium in one block, which we were allowed to play in when the recruits were not in residence. I say play in, as we were not in to fitness training as folks of today. There was plenty of equipment, wall bars, ropes suspended from the ceiling for climbing, wooden box horse, spring board etc. and all without any insurance!!!

During the school holidays, George and I would be allowed to accompany the recruits on their weekly swim at Lancaster swimming baths which had been booked by the Constabulary for a couple of hours a week. This was a period when I was endeavouring to swim a complete circuit under water. I managed it once including the dive. Now I can't remember how long the pool was so it's no big deal.

George, who had been given piano lessons when at Marton and had sacked his teacher, became interested again when his new teacher took the piano to pieces to show him what it was all about, but after a couple of years we moved on and the piano became a heavy piece of furniture. However, at Lancaster George renewed his interest in music and found jazz! He started practising again as some of his classmates at the Lancaster Royal Grammar School had formed a jazz club. This was a time when he was considering himself a cut above the likes of a humble moron like me and wouldn't be seen walking down the street with me. However, his piano playing, became quite good which came in very handy in our teenage years!

On arrival at Lancaster, I was enrolled at Dallas Road Central School under the headship of one Joseph Benson (cruelly nick named Shuffling Joe). He was an excellent headmaster who suffered from severe shell shock from the First World War that caused him to walk with a sort of shuffling motion. His hands were continually shaking but he could write perfectly as the nib of the pen would appear quite still, whilst his hand was shaking. He decided that I was to be put into the 'A' stream for a start and I had no sooner settled there then I was moved up to the Alpha stream. This lot were already studying French so I had some catching up to do. He obviously saw some latent potential in my humble self as he contacted my father with a view to getting a grant from his old Regiment, as he knew that there was money available to educate the children of ex-members. Alas, means testing ruled that out and I happily continued to absorb knowledge at Dallas Road.

The French teacher was a stunning, 22 year old, redhead by the name of Lena Booth. She drove her own car (which was unusual for a woman) and would turn up with a set of skis on the roof of her car on the last day of term. Not many people went skiing in those days especially from the northern counties. I can still sing some of the French ditties that she taught us!

Another teacher I remember was our woodwork and metalwork master. On first entering his class, he would explain that we would be working with very sharp tools. He would teach us how to keep them sharp as blunt tools were dangerous tools. Should we manage to cut ourselves, we would receive first aid treatment and then we would be given the cane for being careless. Lessons which have stood me in good stead for the rest of my days. I am ashamed that I cannot recall his name. Our Form Teacher was Miss Armstrong (Lill). She was a brilliant teacher with a great sense of humour and had a nick name for most of us. I can distinctly remember her tapping me on the head with a ruler whilst leaning over, reading my work, with the remark, "Sandy, you're a true Briton! Troubled with afterthought." I guess I must have made an alteration.

Our sports master was a young teacher called Harry Lancaster. He and Lena Booth would take a party of boys and girls down to the football field further down Dallas Road where we would divide ourselves into two teams and kick a ball around for half an hour or so whilst the girls played hockey. At 4pm we were dismissed on the field and allowed to make our own way home. The lane from our sports field went under a railway bridge and secreted pupils have been aware of two teachers kissing under that bridge. Harry Lancaster was a real handsome guy and a great jazz pianist. After school, some of us would stay behind in the Hall, to listen to him playing a few of the old jazz classics.

If I was in time, I would get to St Mary's Churchyard in time to see The Royal Scot passing through Lancaster station on its way North. This was the crack LMS, record breaking steam train that was the express from London Euston to Glasgow. It did not stop at Lancaster and was reaching its top speed of well over 100 miles per hour as it got to what was known as the Carnforth Flats. This was where the throttle was really open and the smoke and the steam would be laying right back. The stoker would certainly be earning his keep at this speed. It was quite a sight in the early thirties. Alas, a bit like people used to watch Concorde! That lot on the other side of the Pennines had The Flying Scotsman going up to Edinburgh and there was great rivalry between the two.

The mention of stokers reminds me of a tale of my father's, of his days as a railwayman and a story he told us of his trip across the Pennines, stoking a goods train during the night.

Train drivers, especially express drivers, were treated like gods in the days of steam. The aspiration of all small boys was to be a train driver. Usually, they only reached the top level when they were in their forties or fifties.

On this particular night, Father was stoking, i.e. acting as fireman, for this particular driver who had something of a reputation for having things done his way! They set off from Walkden Yard (which was a goods marshalling yard near Manchester) with a goods train mainly loaded with coal. The harder the engine has to work, the more steam has to be generated and of course, it is the fireman's job to shovel coal from the tender, which is behind the footplate where the driver and fireman travel. The driver usually stands on the offside of the cab, leaning out of the offside with his hand on the throttle lever. The cleanliness of the footplate is the responsibility of the fireman. This driver's orders were to "Drop three in the middle and one in each corner". This meant that three shovels full of coal were to be spread in the middle of the firebox and one in each corner. The door to the firebox is opened by a lever which this driver took control of. He refused to open the firebox door until the loaded shovel was on its way to the box, obviously to conserve heat. However, it's a pitch black night. There are no lights on the footplate and Father was being blinded every time the firebox door opened. Consequently, a shovel full of coal catches the edge of the firebox and ends up on the footplate. After much swearing, cleaning up, and getting back to raising steam, the driver still refused to leave the firebox door open until the fuel was ready to be thrown in and repeat performances took place. Father by this time was not a happy man. He managed to stand it until they reached Huddersfield when the train came to a halt. He climbed down from the footplate, turned to the driver and told him that if he wanted to get home he could stoke the b..... thing himself as he had got a lift back home on another train. End of train driving career!

We had a good set of mates in that form, some of the names I recall, Topsy Bains, Plugger alias Joe Cragg,

Muggsy etc. where are they now? The rest escape me! I know Topsy Bains didn't survive the war. I have no idea about the rest and I'm sure there will not be many of that age group on Friends Reunited! As usual, there was the school bully who decided that I was once again to become a target. However, this time he was to get more than he bargained for. He was a tall fat lad who wore glasses. I don't think I ever knew his name. He always had his 'hangers on' around him and on this occasion, decided to pick a fight with me for some reason. It was a challenge, and I decided I was not going to back off. The usual ring formed in the playground, and he removed his glasses and jacket and handed them to his friends. Fists were raised and there was only one punch in it. He charged at me, I stuck out a straight left and caught him right on the bridge of his nose which drew blood and caused him to collapse in tears. It was right where his glasses rested. Two members of staff who were watching from an upstairs window were witnessing all this. We were both sent for to receive a warning for fighting but I can distinctly remember the smile on the teacher's face as she spoke to me, as if to say, "About time that happened to him." I had no further trouble with bullies at Dallas Road!

It was a mixed school and being around 13 I was noticing the girls and had a certain attraction to particular girl called Irene Lines. Her parents had a couple of sweet shops. One down by the river where she lived and another in the main square opposite the museum.

Our route home from school took us past the railway station, around the back of the Castle, through the churchyard where we parted company, Irene carrying on down the lane towards the rugby ground and her home whilst I would return through the churchyard, right around the castle wall to my home. This carried on for some time until I made a date with her to go to a picture house on a Saturday afternoon. I turned up but she didn't. The following Monday, when we got to the parting of the ways,

I told her that I had purchased a ticket for her for the cinema the previous Saturday which I hadn't. She took offence, grabbed a handful of coins out of her purse and threw them at me. They fell in the field by the churchyard wall and we went our separate ways from then on. I later went back and spent some time looking for the cash. I think I found most of it but would have loved a modern metal detector.

Sport became my main interest at Lancaster. I reasoned that if I ran everywhere my speed and stamina would increase. I was unable to wear my pumps to school in the morning as we were given a mark as we entered the classroom on the cleanliness of our shoes. The teacher would stand at the door looking down and she would say, "Ten. Ten. Nine. Eight. Ten." etc. as we walked through the doorway. This was recorded for future privileges. At lunchtime, during the better weather, I ran home and couldn't get my pumps (rubber soled canvas shoes) on fast enough to continue racing around and back to school. It was all part of my leisure activity which at that time was physical training and boxing.

There was a club down Dallas Road known as The Lancaster Lads Club and I used to spend as many evenings as I could down there. It had a small changing room at the far end, then a permanent boxing ring, followed by a gymnasium, then two snooker tables, two table tennis tables and a small office where we could purchase a cup of Bovril for a penny. We young lads would be welcomed by some of the boxers who were boxing professionally at the Morecambe Winter Gardens and elsewhere. As my skill in the ring developed I was offered a fight on the Winter Gardens bill. On informing my mother about it, she hit the roof and promptly put a stop on my aspirations to be world champion!

The number one boxer at our gym was a man who fought under the name of Nippy Howard. He was quite a bit heavier than me and used me as a sparring partner.

On one occasion after we had been sparring for a few rounds, he let fly with a right hook, which was meant to miss, but I walked into it and took it right on the chin. I learned what it was like to be knocked out as my legs turned to rubber and I could no longer stand up. Nippy caught me before I fell and was so sorry as it was not meant to make contact. I soon came round and suffered no ill effect, I think!

My gym work continued and I was able to try my hand at wrestling as we had some coconut mats on the floor. I eventually made the PT display team, which performed at local fetes. This was to be repeated during the early years of my police career when they formed a display team, largely for publicity and recruitment reasons. This Police Display Team came in very handy on one occasion as were returning from a display in Manchester. It would be about the early fifties when a certain amount of anti-Semitism was being demonstrated and our coach was passing through Eccles centre about 7pm. A gang of youths had smashed the shop window of a Jewish store and the local Sergeant and a young Constable were trying to deal with the mob when, out of the blue, a coach load of fit coppers, in civilian clothes, came to their assistance. They didn't know what had hit them, and that includes the Police Officers. We filled Eccles Police Station with prisoners. Fortunately for the local Sergeant, most of them were later released without charge when tempers had cooled. (Perhaps this story should have been included in a later chapter but it seemed to fit in here.)

Another of my friends at that time was the son of the manager of the gas works in Lancaster. Names have deserted me with the passage of time! We used to play in the works grounds during school holidays. The whole place smelled of gas. It must have been escaping from somewhere, but no one seemed to bother, although I cannot recall anyone smoking around the place. There was one huge gasometer, which appeared to be in two sections.

Each section had steel ladders attached to the side. The whole thing was painted green. Not being a lover of heights, I was never tempted to climb those ladders and I cannot imagine having to paint it. When it was full, the upper section would rise to an enormous height and both sections appeared to be floating in water. There was no such thing as North Sea Gas. It had to be manufactured from coal with a by-product of coke that was also a very useful source of fuel. It was coke that was used in all the Nissen hut stoves that heated our billets during the Second World War.

During our stay at Lancaster, the family became mobile! Mother and Father decided to sell off all their assets, except Mum's wedding ring. They raised about a hundred pounds and Father went off to the local Ford Dealers arriving home with a Ford 8hp two door, which were selling for £100 brand new. The salesman asked him if he could drive, gave him a demo around the town, and he turned up at the front door proficient in the art of mastering double declutching etc! I do not think that he had ever driven a vehicle before but had seen it done!

Weekend came around and Father and Mother decided to take us all for a drive and picnic to the Lake District. There was George, age about 16, myself about 13, Joan about 9 in the back and Douglas, who was about 6 sitting on Mother's knee. All went pretty well until we came to a rather steep hill (up Coniston way I think). TJ 575 had only three forward gears and the lowest of these did not have synchromesh. This meant that the speed of the car and the revolutions of the engine had to be synchronised in order for the gear to be engaged. This required a fair degree of skill and practise to execute whilst the car was in motion. Result, gear would not engage. There was much grinding of gears and the car came to a stop. Father managed to pull the handbrake on before we had rolled very far backwards. He was then faced with a hill start on a pretty severe hill. The engine was revved pretty hard, the car leaped several times and stalled. After several attempts it was decided that we would all dismount and allow Father to try on his own having removed the load and perhaps with a little assistance from the stronger members of the family but first, we had to find a suitable stone to scotch the rear wheels. This was successfully carried out and with much pushing and the car leaping, the summit was duly achieved without passengers, who were laboriously following behind and counting their blessings that the weather was fine. We had some trouble with that bottom gear but the art was later mastered and lasted until they bought TJ 6543, a Ford 8hp 4 door about 12 months later. This was a deluxe version costing £120. We had a folding luggage grid attached to the rear of this car that would be piled up with suitcases for our annual trip south to Aldershot. Mother learned to drive on this car but after taking a friend to Sunderland Point, getting caught by the tide when trying to return and having to be rescued, she kind of lost interest! However, as she held her licence before driving tests were required, it remained valid until she took up ambulance driving during the war.

Our trips South became more frequent and somewhat more eventful with having our own transport and six of us in a small Ford with suitcases piled up on the rear luggage rack. On one occasion a bolt came loose and dropped out of its location in the hinge of the luggage rack, with the result that all suitcases trailed on the roadway depositing most of their contents before we were able to stop. This was long before motorways existed so we were not cruising at 70 mph.

About 1932 or 1933, unfortunately my grandfather Beesley died. Mother and Father together with Joan and Douglas went down to the funeral. George and I stayed at home and continued at school. Some time later my grandmother came to live with us and was still with us until just after the war when she died about a couple of years before my mother. Granny was taken south and buried with my grandfather.

George left school about the same time as me, having matriculated at Lancaster Royal Grammar. He tried to get into journalism but failed when they heard his father's occupation as they thought he wouldn't be staying long. He then applied to become a Boy Clerk in the Lancashire Constabulary (what is now a Cadet) and was successful. He was posted to Widnes where he worked in the detective office until joining the Police proper.

Chapter 4

Apprenticeship

In July 1934 Dallas Road School closed for the summer holidays. I was 13 years old and would be 14 before it reopened. The school leaving age then, was 14 so my school days had come to an end! There was no celebration or scenes of elation. I just walked out, never to return.

As, by this time, I was car mad I persuaded my father to try and get me an apprenticeship at the garage where he bought his Fords, Barton Townley's of Lancaster. There was no vacancy in their workshop but they would take me on in the electricians' shop with a view to moving to the workshop when a vacancy was available. The electricians' shop was a part of the overall garage, which contained all the battery replating and charging equipment, a long bench with a stone sink at one end and an acetylene cylinder at the other, which was connected to a blowtorch. This was used for melting the lead terminals when replating. Alongside the sink was a set of wooden steps that led to the upholsterer's shop and the place where we ate our lunch. Much leg pulling and horse play went on on the upholsterer's table and we lads came in for a lot of it! The upholsterer, who's name I believe was Arthur, would sing to me at least once a day, "Tommy lad, Tommy lad, though you're scarce a wee, you're old." I have no idea where it comes from and I have never heard it since. [It comes from a song called "Tommy Lad" by Vernon Dalhart 1917.] I met Arthur many years later as I left a hangar at Cosford School of Technical Training whilst serving in the RAF. He was a civilian instructor in the art of repairing airframes. Some were in fact made of fabric in those days and still are in the old classics.

My first job was learning how to replate batteries. As the batteries came in, they had to have the sulphuric acid drained from them into the sink. After drilling and removing the external lead connectors, the battery would then be placed in the electric oven until the pitch melted; a special puller would be applied and the old plates removed from each cell in turn. The old lead plates were thrown under the sink until there was sufficient to have removed. Any acid, which failed to drain into the sink, appeared to be absorbed by my overalls as they quickly became perforated by little holes with red edges. The new plates and separators were assembled into their respective compartments and new covers were sealed with hot pitch. The connectors were joined with molten lead run into a small steel mould. It took a while to get the temperature right, as if it was too hot all the lead would run away and there would be much verbal instruction and character assassination. The electrician, under whose instruction I was employed was an excellent bloke and we got on very well and I enjoyed my time with him which was about 12 months. My wage was five shillings a week (old money). If I worked an hour overtime I would get an extra penny. They kept 2d out of my wage to pay for a stamp. (What sort of a stamp I've no idea.) I don't know how much my mother paid for my overalls but she assured me that she was out of pocket even when I paid her the lot!

During my time in this department, I was given a job to rewire a hand lamp or inspection lamp. This consisted of a three-pin plug at one end of a length of three-core cable, a bulb holder at the other, the bulb being surrounded by a wire cage. The plug was already attached and I was to wire up the lamp end. I was told where to put the red and black wires in the bulb holder and the green wire was to be connected to a bolt on the wire cage, this being the earth.

After following these instructions, I carried the lamp over to the sink area, stood on the old lead plates, plugged it in and switched on. I got the full 230 volts through the wire cage which I was clutching in my hand and I remember my whole body shaking. I was unable to release it as my muscles were paralysed. I fell backwards scraping my arm on some house batteries which were standing behind me and fortunately the hand lamp flew out of my hand. I don't remember much more apart from being taken home and given the following day off. I sure am lucky to be here to tell this story!

Another hair raising moment was when the electrician had to go up on the flat roof to repair a neon sign and he needed a helper. Now, the one thing that I am not happy about is heights! I had no trouble climbing up there, but getting over the parapet to get my feet on the ladder was quite another matter. I was up there for ages (or so it seemed) before I could make the move to descend. I have no problem with flying but standing on high buildings and tall ladders is just not for me and I have managed to keep my feet on the ground as much as possible ever since.

Whilst I enjoyed about 12 months in the electrical department, my aim was to get out into the workshop. The person i/c of the garage was a Mr Teddy Townley, the brother of the big boss Barton Townley, so I put it to him that he was missing out on the best apprentice around and he agreed to me working with one of his top men. However, my first job was to clean the engine of the boss's car. At the time, he was running a 41/2 litre, coach built Lagonda. A beautiful motorcar. It was a pleasure to clean and I gave it the works. High-pressure paraffin spray and plenty of metal polish. Most of the engine was polished aluminium and all the metal piping was either copper or brass. I spent most of a whole day on it and it really did look great. I later heard that he couldn't stop lifting the bonnet to let people view his showpiece.

Ford, at this time, was giving a good deal of publicity to their promise to exchange an engine for a reconditioned one in a day. Bring it in in the morning and take it home at night with a new engine. Townleys, being a main agent, were charged with setting up an engine reconditioning bay and my mechanic, a guy by the name of Tom Whitehead, and I worked in this bay whenever we hadn't been allocated another job. The bay consisted of a special caged off section of the workshop, which was lockable, as many special tools were required to carry out the reconditioning as per Ford's instructions. When vehicles came in with special problems, we would sometimes be given the job and one I still remember is fitting new distributor points to a Ford V8 Coupe. In particular, I remember the test drive afterwards. The acceleration of these vehicles was fantastic. There were only three forward gears but the V8 propelled the vehicle forward, up to about 50 or 60 mph, at an alarming rate. This sowed the seed for an unattained ambition to be a racing car technician. Maybe, if I had been able to stay there, there might have been a chance, as one of Barton's sons had bought a racing M.G. and was starting to compete in motor racing events.

Incidentally, the Ford V8 engine mentioned above became one of the main power plants for a huge number of Second World War vehicles.

The general stores was also a caged off area where spares and special tools were kept. This had a flat roof where new tyres were stored. It was a favourite place for apprentices to skive and some have even been known to take forty winks after a heavy night!

One such character was called Bailey. Many years later, about 15/20, I was on traffic duty at Haydock Park Races. After the traffic was all in and parked, we would go and watch some of the races. As I approached the Grand Stand, Bailey came up to me and said, "Don't I know you?" He had survived the war and had brought a coach party down from Lancaster. It was good to see one of the old workmates.

However, I digress. The apprenticeship at Townleys was coming to a close as Father's time at the Castle was almost up and I was not earning enough to keep myself in fags never mind digs. I would be about 16 when the move came through. Pictures were down again and we were off to Leigh.

Chapter 5

Leigh

Leigh was a typical Lancashire industrial town of coal mining and cotton spinning. Our house was in Chapel Street, which was the road leading out of town towards Butts Bridge and Manchester. We lived in a street, next door to a car showroom that did not seem to do much business. My brother Douglas and his family later occupied this house. Mother was not used to living in an industrial Lancashire town and I remember her shedding many tears at this latest posting. She did not go out to work as most women do nowadays and on one occasion she decided to clean the outside of the front windows. A few doors away from us, towards the town centre, was a fish and chip shop. A lorry driver, who had been making a delivery, shouted out of his cab as he drove away, "Ger int' corners Ma!" Mother felt humiliated and never cleaned an outside window again!

As I was now unemployed, I was obliged to sign on at the 'dole office'. Being then about 16 I was required to attend a 'dole school' where I decided to learn shorthand for some unearthly reason. I didn't get very far with it. I think I learned the first part of the alphabet and found it very boring so I got myself a job as a second man on a goods lorry.

A few hundred yards towards the town from our house, was a small garage. Three petrol pumps and a couple of oil tanks. It had a small workshop and an inspection pit. Across the other side of Chapel Street, were two bakeries side by side. An entrance at the side of each of these led to a yard where the goods vehicles of a firm called

Hesfords were kept and maintained. Hesfords also had a small warehouse in Sugar Lane, Manchester. Most of their transport business was delivering to and from the mills of Lancashire and Yorkshire; skips full of bobbins and huge beams of woven material, bales of cloth wrapped in brown paper, together with general goods such as sides of bacon wrapped in mutton cloth, cheeses and general boxed goods mainly for grocers. For some time, I rode with one of the drivers, helping in the deliveries. It was pretty hard work and involved some heavy lifting. One minute I would be sweating and the next freezing. The firm did not pay me as I tagged along of my own free will but I got a tip from the drivers and one taught me to drive the lorry around the yard and in the mill yards. That was a 31/2-ton Albion. After a few weeks of this I managed to get a job with the little garage, which was then owned, by a father and son by the name of Sutcliffe. The garage was used by the Hesford fleet to refuel each evening. The idea was to try and carry on with the apprenticeship that I had started. Unfortunately, there were no paper qualifications at that time, so it was just a case of getting as much experience as one could and progressing up the pay scale.

The Sutcliffes however, did not have a very good sense for business and the garage was going down hill. They eventually went broke and I was once again out of work. Fortunately, one of the Hesford brothers took on the garage and we were back in business. As well as helping in the workshop, I was often required to serve petrol etc. We had three hand pumps. These were operated by turning a handle, lifting a gallon of petrol into a glass chamber at the top of the pump and while the handle was being unwound, the fuel would run into the vehicle's tank. Then the whole process would be repeated for the next gallon and so on. This was a laborious job when the lorries came in and wanted 20 gallons or so. However, whilst I was there, the boss purchased three second hand electric pumps and once these were installed we thought our troubles were over. It was certainly easier but one day, one of the pumps caught fire. The electric motor had evidently over heated and burst into flames. It was panic stations as there was about 600 gallons under that pump. After calling the fire brigade we managed to get the metal covers off the pump and got the fire out with sand and an extinguisher before the arrival of the brigade. It could all have turned out so different!

Whilst working upstairs at this garage (the lathe and drilling machines were up there together with a load of scrap metal and spare parts) I came across a piece of solid brass about 9" long and 1" x 11/2" section. I saw a model of a racing Alfa Romeo in that and it duly became the brass model that adorns our china cabinet. [See front cover] Unfortunately, my knowledge of metals was not as good as it could have been as one of the suspension spats and the driver's headrest, which are soldered on, turned out to be phosphor bronze but no one appears to have noticed. It was not completed until well after the war when Dennis Taylor moved in next-door when we lived at Failsworth. He had a modelling lathe and we were able to get the wheels turned.

A family called Green ran one of the bakeries across from the garage. Their son Harry and I became the best of friends. Brother George was still working in the detective office at Widnes and was travelling back and forth on a motorcycle that Granny had bought for him. This was a New Imperial 150cc, which caused me no end of trouble as the timing kept slipping and we would be stripping it down in the kitchen very other night. It was later changed for a B.S.A. 250cc, which was a much better machine. I have travelled many miles on the pillion of that B.S.A. even slept on the way back from Lancaster one night and lost all the magazines that I was supposed to be looking after.

On George's bike

George and I went all over the place on that bike. One of our favourite runs on a Sunday was around the Horseshoe Pass in North Wales. Beautiful scenery and lovely roads. I once got left behind in Chester. I used to wear a rubber riding coat, which fastened around my legs. As we waited at the traffic lights, which were red, I stood up to make myself more comfortable, not paying attention to the lights. The lights change to green, he let the clutch in and I'm standing there shouting, "Wait for me!" He did, but wasn't very pleased.

We had a few friends with motorcycles at Leigh. On one occasion, Harry Green, on the pillion of one of his mate's bike and George and me on the BSA went out one evening in the summer for a country run. We stopped somewhere and George let me have a go on the bike with Harry on the pillion. We ran out of road on a bend, hit a grass bank and I went over the handlebars and head first into the grass bank. Harry went over my head and into a thorn bush. We did not wear crash helmets in those days and I split the top of my head. Poor Harry was a mass of thorns, which we were pulling out of his face and head weeks later. The story was that George was riding with me on the pillion, the front brake cable became detached and as we headed for the bank, Harry, in jumping out of the way had to leap into the thorn bush.

After straightening out the handlebars and front forks we headed home with me clutching a handkerchief to my head and blood streaming down my face. What a shock my mother got when she saw me looking over the back yard gate. They whipped me off to hospital in Leigh where the night sister cleaned me up shaved the top of my scalp and inserted a row of stitches. I had to return in 10 days time to have them removed. This I duly did and George and I set off from the hospital for Poole, Bournemouth for a week's holiday with some relatives of my mother, whom I have never seen since.

When my birthday came around Granny decided that she would buy me a present and I asked for a trumpet. We subsequently bought a Dearman Wornal which I still have. George was still playing piano, I was getting the old lips back in the groove and Harry Green's dad had bought him a set of drums. We were the boys in those days. Trilby hat and a pipe. (I was 16 and could smoke officially!) Mother used to buy me 20 fags on her grocery order every week.

There was not a lot to do for young people on a Sunday in Leigh. No cinemas or sports took place on a Sunday but Sunday evening, the youth of the town would dress up in their finery and parade along the main street, up and down, up and down. All hoping to chat up someone of the opposite sex. It never worked for me or my mates but we were not discouraged as we would all be there again the following Sunday. This seemed to be a regular happening in Lancashire as I was later to discover! It was known as the local 'monkey run'.

Our little trio was progressing a treat and we were getting quite a programme together. A contact of Harry's heard about us and came along to sing. He had a good voice and could also sing some of the old trad. jazz numbers. Alas, it all came to an end when the pictures were down again and we were off to Darwen. I have since heard that our singer, who's name I cannot recall, did not survive the war. What a waste of human talent is war!!

Chapter 6

Darwen

Darwen was another typical Lancashire town which consisted mainly of the main A666 running between Blackburn and Bolton and on towards Manchester, with steep streets rising off on either side. Its main industries apart from the cotton mills were paint manufacture and paper making, in particular, wallpaper, Crown paints and Walpamur wall papers.

We lived in Bold Venture Road I think, then it might have been Borough Road, at the bottom of which was a small garage owned and run by the Holden family. I soon made myself known to them and obtained work with the resident mechanic in the workshop which held about four or five cars when tightly packed. There was a showroom alongside, which would hold another four or five. The main business was car dealing and we were employed to make them 'serviceable' for sale. Holden senior had connections down in London and we occasionally took a trip down to drive cars back. These were usually of the hearse type or large taxi, Austin 20's.

By this time, I had turned 17 and was of an age to start driving legally. Father owned a Ford 10hp at this time and I was obliged to take a driving test, as they had just become law. I applied, and took my first test in Burnley. I don't remember too much about it but I know why I failed. I was required to reverse into the hovel of a disused warehouse. I distinctly remember that the rounded kerbs were steel clad. This was common practise to prevent the steel tyres of the horse drawn carts from breaking up the kerb edges when being backed in. I caught the kerb with the rear wheel and failed.

My next test took place in Bolton. My father was convinced that I had failed the first by driving too fast. He drilled it into me that I was to drive real slowly for my second. I didn't get out of second gear for ages and when I did get into top the examiner said, "I want to see you use that gear more." I did and I passed!

Above the garage, was a workshop which was entered by a flight of wooden steps from alongside the showroom. This was used by a family by the name of Isherwood, who's business was the manufacture of printing rolls for use in the wallpaper industry. The wooden rollers were made up of designs that were copied in brass strips which were set into the roller, edge on, and the centres were filled tightly with felt. It appeared to be a highly skilled job involving an enormous degree of patience. Their tools mainly consisted of dozens of differently shaped pliers and cutters. The finished article would then be taken to the printers for use in their machines. I got to know the two sons of the family very well as they lived a few doors up the road from us and the younger son, I think he was called Reg, became one of my best friends for a while. Unfortunately, the labour involved in the making of these rollers and the speed at which they could be manufactured, could not keep up with the requirements of the industry and new methods of printing were developed. Consequently, the business closed down and the family moved down to the Midlands where I believe, Reg went working at the Rover works in Birmingham.

As the upper workshop became empty, Holden senior decided that we would sink a hydraulic lift in the area of the steps then we would be able to raise the vehicles, swing them around and drive them through the double doors into the upstairs workshop as working conditions would be much better there where it was warmer and dryer. We all started work on the hole digging and eventually had the lift installed. It was quite a precarious operation driving a vehicle off the lift and into the workshop and one can imagine what it was like driving one out of the workshop and onto the two ramps to bring it down. We never had one off the ramps whilst I was working there. I wonder what the Safety at Work people would say about that operation nowadays.

The mechanic that I worked with at that time had some sort of a falling out with the boss and packed his job in. He was a decent bloke, bred budgies as a hobby and was quite famous in the show circles. However, he was able to get a job with a local taxi firm who were also funeral directors and wedding specialists. They owned a fleet of Rolls Royce taxis, a Rolls Royce hearse and a big Ford Lincoln ambulance.

Holden also had a scrap yard and would buy or scrounge anything that he thought he could make a bob or two out of. He had some sort of a contract with the paint manufacturers to take excess or contaminated varnish and this would be dumped in the scrap yard in barrels. In quiet times in the garage, he would expect me to take out an old Leyland lorry to convey these barrels about and I objected to this as I considered this was not part of my job. Result, we had a row and I told him what he could do with his job! I contacted my old mate at the taxi firm and joined him in maintaining the fleet etc.

Holden junior, by the name of Gilbert was about 5 or 6 years older than me. He was a bit of an M.G. enthusiast and at times we would have a couple for sale. Needless to say, a good deal of time was spent tuning these and we often had a little blitz around the place. We were once caught by my father racing down our road in them. We were severely chastised and considered ourselves very lucky!

Whilst working for the Holdens I came into contact with some strange characters. One in particular was a guy known as Little Titch. He was about 5' tall and sometimes immaculate. He would turn up in a well cut suit, driving a Rolls or some other posh motor, with his dollybird of a wife dressed up beside him. He would literally sell the shirt off his back if he could make a profit and I have seen him arrive at the garage with nothing, even wearing a pair of his wife's shoes. He said that he had sold his own but I suspect that his wife had thrown him out without them or that she had pawned them. I once visited the flat in Manchester where they lived and what a tip! Enough said about that.

Cars that were not too good mechanically that had been taken in part exchange and would be uneconomic to repair, would be sold off at a car auction in Manchester. One of the rules of the auction was that cars had to be driven in. It was known that repairs have been bodged and I have been on the back end of a tow rope to about 200 yards from the auction, tow rope stowed away, and the car driven in on trade plates. They were dishonest traders and I was glad to leave despite the fact that my girl friend worked in the office! (More about my love life will be included in the final chapter which will only be written should my beloved wife Catherine predecease me.) There were some very dodgy practises carried on in the motor trade in those days. I think it is a little better today but I would never trust them! (Saw dust in gearboxes mixed with the oil to deaden the noise of worn bearings etc. I heard of big end bearings being silenced with bacon rind being clamped between the crankshaft and the bearing caps.) This wouldn't happen today as designs have changed.

Recreation at this time was mainly dancing and swimming. The trumpet was also a hobby which was beginning to bear fruit and I was taking lessons with a lead trumpeter in the Eddy McGarry (Broadcasting) Band which was currently playing at one of the top dance halls in the area, The Accrington Conservative Club. I was practising riffs from one of the greatest jazz trumpeters of our times, Bunny Berigan. I remember the book well, it had a maroon cover and was beginning to become worn (it disappeared during the war) when events overtook the lessons. Father was promoted to the rank of Inspector and transferred to Orrell outside Wigan. When the pictures came down this time, I decided to remain in Darwen and was offered accommodation with another mate called Stanley Knowles. I stayed with Stan and his mother and father in Greenway Street. Stan was working in the office of a mill in Blackburn. His father worked in a paper making factory and took me in to show me how they made rolls of paper for newspapers. The finished article was a huge roll, wrapped in brown paper and it must have weighed about a ton. The heat in there was overwhelming unless you were used to it. I think they got a beer allowance to put all the sweat back.

I was now earning enough to pay for my digs but had to rely on my parents for the trumpet lessons. Things were going well in that respect. I went along with my tutor to the Melody Maker presentation night in Blackburn, which is the big night when all the local musicians get together and was about to be taken along to the Eddy McGarry band when funds dried up and the lessons had to cease. At this time, I was involved with one Ethel Wolstenholme of Great Harwood and life was rather hectic.

It was whilst living with the Knowles' that I started with a series of boils on my arms. I don't know whether it was the change of diet or some sort of contamination but as soon as the centre of one was cleared, another would break out. Mrs. Knowles used to bathe them with hot water and pink lint. I eventually went to my doctor who took some blood, sent it away and had a serum made up which he injected back in to my arm. I don't known what it was but it seemed to do the trick as they eventually cleared up and I have never been troubled since.

Our best dance venue in Darwen during the winter was the local swimming baths. It was quite a new building. There was a large swimming pool with a stage at one end and tiered seats on either side where spectators would sit to watch water polo matches during the summer. Come the winter, the pool would be boarded over and hired out to whoever wanted to run a dance. There were good catering facilities and it was always used for the Police Ball. Another of our special nights was New Years Eve. One year, when New Years Day fell on a Monday there was a problem with the licence as there were no licences for dancing on a Sunday. So the organisers held it commencing at midnight and we celebrated the New Year first and carried on until the wee small hours of the morning. Then home for a fry up!

There were usually four or five of us in the gang that I used to knock about with, Reg was one, another was Stanley Knowles. There was always a dance to attend on a Saturday night. Then we had the theatre in Blackburn which was only a tram ride away. There was usually a music hall show there, all the stand up comics and tap dancers. There was one act which became quite famous. It was two guys and a girl known as Wilson, Kepple and Betty. They were dressed as Arabs, never smiled and came on to the stage spreading a bag of sand into a large tray which they then climbed into and went into the soft shoe sand dance to the tune of "The Sheik of Araby" They were brilliant! The show always opened and closed with a troupe of girls high kicking and dancing in a chorus line.

During 'wakes week' (that is the week's annual holiday when all the mills and factories close down) a group of us lads would set off for Cunninghams Camp in Douglas on the Isle of Man. This was an all male camp. It was called a camp but there were no tents. The accommodation was quite good. As it was on the top of the cliff, there was an escalator which ran until 11pm. This took one up to the reception lounge which was beautifully set out with plants, mainly palms and a fountain. There was a dance hall which was in full swing by 11am and went on all day and evening. I don't know where all the girls came from but there were plenty.

We also visited the Isle of Man to watch the TT Races. Gilbert Holden and I went over one year. I think it was 1938. I know it was before the Japanese bikes had arrived and Norton were winning everything. Gilbert always had a car so we could do it in a day. Drive to Liverpool, catch the early morning boat, watch the races in the afternoon and return on an evening boat back to Liverpool. A tiring day but well worth it! Many years later, I came across Gilbert running a three pump filling station on the A59 at Langho and living with his wife in a bungalow next door.

Chapter 7

"Peace in our time?"

The year would be about 1938 and I remember the Prime Minister of the time, Neville Chamberlain returning from Munich, waving a piece of paper, which was supposed to be from Hitler saying, "Peace in our time!" or words to that effect. I was sitting at the table at home in Orrell and we were all listening to the six o'clock news. I was playing with the clip of a meat paste bottle, bending it until it broke, which it did, and lacerated my right thumb from the nail to my wrist. Fortunately, my father was at home who gave me first aid to try and stop the bleeding and we went down to the doctor's surgery where he pinned the wound together with metal clips. The scar is still with me!

After my altercation with Holden senior, and moving a few hundred yards across the main road to join my former partner at the taxi firm, my education was to be expanded rather rapidly. As the firm were also undertakers, I was able to work overtime by driving a funeral car and assisting with the removal of bodies, coffins etc. As long as I was wearing dark trousers, they would lend me a black overcoat and a peaked cap and I would follow the hearse with the grieving relatives. To pick them up, would involve helping the funeral director, who sat in the passenger seat of the hearse and the hearse driver to load the coffin into the hearse. This was done with great solemnity as the coffin was often resting on our chromium trestle in the front room. The family would then pay their last respects. The lid would be put on the coffin and a young boy in the family would screw down the lid. He would give each screw a couple of turns and we would finish it off. I don't know whether it was a religious ritual or whether it was particular to that part of Lancashire. It didn't always happen but quite often. We were often given a glass of sherry just to be sociable. We would drive in procession to the church and act as pallbearers if necessary, then take the mourners to wherever they were having refreshment. I was once told not to drive them back so fast as they would think that we were trying to get rid of them.

When not taxi driving, we were engaged in the maintenance of some quite old Rolls Royces. The hearse was a 40/50 conversion, the engine of which was in beautiful condition. It had a dual ignition system. One set of sparking plugs would be fired by a magneto and the other by coil ignition. The ignition timing was controlled by a lever on the steering wheel. Quite often, when starting it in the morning, merely by moving the lever on the steering wheel back to the retard position, then pushing it up to the advanced position, it would cause the magneto to spark one of the plugs and the engine would burst into life on the mixture that had been stored in the cylinder over night. I have never experienced this since in any vehicle.

Attached to the garage was a joiners' shop where the coffins were made and the bodies were fitted with the shroud, laid in the coffin and made presentable. All the coffins were lined with a kind of pitch in order to prevent leakage in transit and considerable care was taken to ensure that the body looked as 'nice' as possible. Sometimes, newspaper was placed around the body under the shroud to keep it in place and fill in the gaps so that it would look nice and smooth on the top.

The undertaking business seemed rather competitive. If a sudden death occurred, there would be great competition to get the body. Tips and retainers to professionals were not unheard of. Being first on the scene was important, as I was later to realise when I joined the police service.

One evening, a couple of staff were going to bring in the body of a 22 stone woman and they asked me if I would like to come along and give them a hand. I had no idea what a 22 stone woman looked like, let alone a dead one. However, we got to the house with the 'box', which is used to carry bodies in transit before being measured for the coffin, and took it into the house. We were then informed that the body was in the front bedroom. As the box was too big to handle up the stairs and over the banister rail, it was decided to bring her down in a sheet. Fortunately, all the members of the family left us to it and kept away downstairs. She was huge! We rolled her onto the sheet and took a blanket as well. We got her onto the landing when the sheet and blanket split down the middle and she ended up on the floor. Eventually, we got the box to the top of the stairs, loaded her in it, and slid it down the stairs and out into the hearse. The carpenters did a super job and she looked remarkably good in the Chapel of Rest. I eventually attended that funeral and instead of bearers, the coffin was wheeled into church on our chromium collapsible trolley. After we had finally disposed of the body we found that the trolley was so twisted and distorted that we could easily have had another disaster.

We also had an ambulance at this firm. Before the days of the National Health Service, anyone needing to go to hospital would have to arrange their own transport unless it was an emergency, when the fire service usually provided that cover. Our ambulance, which was a big Lincoln, American vehicle and must have weighed a couple of tons, was mainly used as a taxi for out patients who required to lie down or were wheelchair bound. I remember taking it out one morning when most of the traffic was unable to move due to a heavy fall of snow during the night. An old lady needed to go to Blackburn Infirmary for treatment and the old Lincoln was about the only vehicle that could have got to her address as it was up a hill. (There were no 4x4s then.)

She and her family were most grateful when we pulled up at her front door.

The affair with the Wolstenholme girl was getting serious. I had been to meet her parents and she was pushing to get engaged. Things were happening in Europe, gas masks were being issued, black out regulations were being ordered but war had not yet been declared.

Chapter 8

Call up

The war clouds were gathering. Black outs were being ordered. Gas masks were being issued and children were being evacuated from the cities. Travelling without lights was pretty grim. Masks were made to cover the headlights of cars and these hardly allowed any light to escape. All railway stations were blacked out and the waiting rooms were dark, smoke filled, smelly places, usually with some troops lying about on the floor, sleeping. As all the trains were pulled by steam locomotives there was always plenty of coal about and the waiting rooms invariably had a huge fire burning. Everyone seemed to smoke. Prior to this period, it was 'not the done thing' for a woman to smoke in public and as for going into a bar, well that was the action of a 'loose woman'. The war certainly changed all that. All streetlights were off and everywhere was in total darkness unless there was a moon. There seemed to be uniform everywhere. The army reservists were called up and conscription was law. Most entertainments carried on as normal. We still went dancing and the theatres and cinemas remained open. Much propaganda was put out over the radio and on the cinema screens urging everyone to carry their gas masks with them and this also became law. Food rationing was ordered and Identity Cards issued.

All sorts of morale boosting songs were written. The French had an 'impenetrable' fortification known as the Maginot Line along its borders with Germany. Similarly, Germany had fortified their borders with the Siegfried Line.

These were huge, concrete gun emplacements with underground tunnels joining them together. The line of one song included that fact that we were going to hang out our washing on it without Hitler's permission. It all sounds so stupid now. But one must remember, we were very parochial in the late 30's. Things like central heating in homes, double glazing and insulation were things of the future and as for television, well we had heard that it was possible to transmit pictures and that the BBC had actually done it but it was more science fiction for we northerners. Few people travelled abroad and those who did, like our French teacher Lena Booth, were the talk of the school, turning up on the last day of term with skis on the top of her car. Unheard of!!

A coal fire, usually in the living room, heated our homes although some houses with two rooms down stairs actually had a fireplace in each. A certain amount of heat was transmitted to the bedrooms through which the chimney passed. Some bedrooms also had fireplaces. These would only be used if someone were sick. These coal fires produced large amounts of thick black soot, which stuck to the chimneys and built up in time and if the chimney was not swept it would often catch fire. Due to the excessive heat in the chimney, a terrific up draught was caused and this resulted in flames, soot and sparks shooting out of the chimney pots on the roof. It was usual for the fire brigade to be called out and what a mess they used to leave behind. Also the local policeman would attend with his note book, as it was a punishable offence. Some people have been known to stick newspaper up the chimney and set light to it as it was cheaper than hiring the services of a chimney sweep and if the chimneys were not cleared out, the fire would not draw properly and there would be falls of soot. Not only that, but a chimney fire contravened the black out as clouds of smoke, sparks and sometimes flames and soot would puther from the chimney.

Multiply the number of properties in a city with the number of coal fires puthering out smoke and one can get some idea of the pollution caused. When atmospheric conditions were at a certain level, this pollution would turn into fog or smog as some called it. Whatever it was called, it reduced visibility to virtually zero. Headlights reflected back at one and were of no use. Some cars were fitted with fog lights low down to try and penetrate beneath the fog but were just about as useless. The fog lights on present day cars are just a selling gimmick as they are used more to warn of the presence of the vehicle when headlights would be better.

Petrol was rationed and only supplied to essential users, so private motoring became a thing of the past although there always seemed to be a few coupons floating about that essential users didn't need. The majority of people did not have private cars and most of one's shopping was done at the local stores or mobile shops would visit remote areas.

Few people had refrigerators and no one had a freezer as far as I know. Most houses had a pantry, usually attached to the kitchen, where food was stored for a short while. Meat was usually kept in a 'meat safe' which was a wooden cupboard, the front doors of which were made of zinc mesh which allowed the air to circulate and prevented the entry of flying insects. Shopping had therefore to be carried out regularly. Supermarkets were things of the future!

As ration books were issued, coupons had to be used to purchase certain foods like meat, eggs, butter (or fats, as they were known). If one went away from home the ration book had to go too. There soon developed a black market where certain goods could be obtained without coupons. Fiddles in stock control or despatched goods that went missing usually supplied these. But on the whole, it seemed to work fairly well. I, personally, never remember feeling hungry but it must have been a nightmare trying to cater for a family.

At this time, my involvement with the said Ethel Wolstenholme was continuing. She was employed by the Holdens and worked in their office. We would meet in Blackburn and do our courting at the various dance halls in the district and sometimes at the local swimming baths. The blackout came in handy at times.

All reservists had been called up and conscription was made compulsory. Occasionally, I would travel home to Orrell where my parents were living, sometimes taking Ethel with me. On the weekend of 3rd of September 1939 I was at home on my own, when war was declared against Germany. George, being in the Police, was in a reserved occupation. Joan and Douglas were still at school so I was the one at the age to be called up. I continued working in Darwen until April 1940.

By this time we were suffering air raids. My Grandmother lived in Eccles, Manchester and had been issued with an Anderson Shelter. This consisted of corrugated iron sheets with a curved corrugated iron roof. The instructions were to dig a deep hole, line it with the metal sheets and put the curved sheets over the top then cover it with the excavated soil. At the sound of the sirens to denote the arrival of a raid, she and my Aunt Matilda (who lived with her) would gather their treasured possessions and retire to the shelter which was situated in the back garden. They spent many nights in that shelter during the blitz on Manchester. Just as well as the pub at the bottom of their street, St James Street, took a direct hit.

Prior to receiving my call up papers, I decided that to continue in my trade, I would apply to join the RAF. I went to the recruiting office in Wigan and signed on the dotted line. "Come in" they said. "Drop your trousers, cough!" And I was in. They said, "Go home and await a call from us." This came after a few weeks and I was given a railway pass to report at RAF Station Wilmslow for basic training. I was given a trade test as a result of which I became

995725 A/C 2 Thomas Sanderson, was kitted out with uniform, underclothes, and shirts, webbing etc. and told to report to a corporal in a certain hut. This was the start of 3 weeks basic training. I think it was three weeks, it certainly seemed longer!

995725 A/C2

The corporal, who's name I cannot remember, was a PTI (Physical Training Instructor). I think they had all been recruited from the ranks of professional boxing or footballers. There was a considerable amount of bull.... with competition between the various flights. Boots had to be spit and polished until you could see your face in the toe caps. All the brass buckles of the webbing and backpacks together with tunic buttons and badges had to be polished. Bed spaces had to be immaculate with the blankets folded and stacked in a certain way so that they measured a certain number of inches, measured with a stick. All the kit was laid out for inspection on the bed in a certain order. It was excellent training for anyone and I retain some of the lessons to this day. All civilian kit was sent home and for the next six years I would be wearing RAF uniform. We were not allowed out of camp for the first week or so, as they wanted to be sure that we would not disgrace the uniform. On leaving the camp for the first time, somehow my belt buckle had got reversed, the end of the belt being on the right instead of the left. As I reached the Guardroom by the gate a voice bellowed, "You, Airman! Do you think that you are a bloody WAAF? Get in here and get that belt on properly." I've never made that mistake since!

Early rising and PT every morning was getting us fit. Then it's on to the parade ground for drill. Marching up and down the parade ground, saluting to the front, about turn, squad will move to the right, open order march, etc. etc. We were then issued with rifles, short Lee-Enfields, 303 calibre which had been used in the First World War, all the commands were centred about these. After many 'ordering arms', 'slope arms', 'for inspection', 'port arms', 'Royal salute' etc. marching up and down with them, we finally got to pulling them to pieces and loading them with dummy ammunition.

There's always one in every squad, or so I'm told. We had one whose father was a Regimental Sergeant Major in the Army. He couldn't work out his right from his left. He would start to march with left leg and left arm together, the poor bloke got shouted at practically every drill. We felt quite sorry for him until we were taken to the firing range at Squires Gate. We had received the drill on loading live ammunition, had fired several rounds at the 100 yards targets and were given the command, "Unload rifles." The drill is then to port arms, i.e. bring the rifle across your chest and work the bolt backwards and forwards several times to show that the breach is empty. The order was then given, "Safety catches on!" The little safety catch behind the bolt is pulled back. This means that the trigger cannot be operated. All of a sudden there was a WEEEEE as a round was fired off into the air whilst the Flight Sergeant was standing in front of us. The air turned blue! Yes, it was our RSM's son. Poor lad! I never knew where he eventually went as the live firing was at the end of our basic training. I, along with many others, was transferred to Blackpool.

Chapter 9

RAF Basic Training

July 1940 Blackpool

TOM SANDERSON

We were transported to Blackpool and allocated billets in what were holiday boarding houses, ruled over by the typical 'Blackpool Landlady'. We were given certain rules on the times we were to be home, as the door would be locked at 11pm. If we were in early enough, she would sell us a cup of cocoa for a penny. My billet was in Central Drive, not far from Central Station. It has all been redeveloped now. Central Station is now a car park. We were given instructions to parade in a certain street at 9am and were marched with many other flights to the huge multi-story car park at Talbot Road. This had been taken over by the RAF and turned into a huge training school for all types of trades.

Our flight was assembled on the third floor and it was here that our futures were to be determined. We were divided into 'airframes' and 'engines'. "You, you and you, over there." We were split into classes of about 12 individuals at random and I was directed to the 'airframes' lot but managed to act the stupid one by getting in the wrong lot. As they didn't know which of us was in the wrong lot, I managed to remain with the 'engines' group.

The next two weeks consisted of basic training, learning to use files, hack saws, surface plates, scribers etc. and we were given a piece of steel to make into an accurate object of a specific dimension. This involved an awful lot of filing, causing many blisters but at the end of a couple of weeks it turned into the finished article which as far as I remember was a solid pyramid with a couple of holes in it. Whilst this was taking place, we were given lectures in things such as the identification of metals etc. We were also given certain definitions to learn. I can still remember the odd one like 'inertia', 'the tendency of a body when at rest to remain at rest'. Now I wonder why that one stuck?

Extract from handwritten and illustrated note book

For the next few weeks we were stripping down engines, learning about radial engines, Bristol Pegasus, Rolls Royce Merlins etc. ignition systems, magnetos, supercharging etc. etc. It was all very interesting. This continued until the final week when we were taken to Squires Gate Airport where we actually came into contact with real aircraft.

We were taught how to handle aircraft. How to refuel them. Made aware of the dangers of static electricity and how everything that came into contact with the plane has first to be earthed. How to picket them down in rough weather. What good lessons these turned out to be!

During this course, Blackpool was full of RAF members on different courses. There must have been thousands of them, including Poles and Ukrainians who had managed to escape to Britain before being captured by the German Forces. The Tower and The Winter Gardens were open and in full swing. We had swimming parades once a week, when we would have to parade in our particular street with our kit, have a roll call and be marched along the front at Blackpool to the Derby Baths, which appeared to have been commandeered for the duration. It was usually dark when we commenced the march. We were in columns of three and the rearmost outside members were given a red paraffin storm lamp to carry to protect us from being mown down by passing vehicles. The column would be about 30 or 40 yards long when we set off. It was soon noted that there was no roll call at the Baths and the column had reduced to half its length by the time that we got there. I never dropped out as I enjoyed the swim and it was a superb swimming baths for its day!

Pay-day was on every other Saturday morning and it took place at the Winter Gardens. As an AC Plonk (as the bottom grade was known) I was getting paid two shillings per day. I.e. twenty-eight shillings per fortnight. (Old money mind!) To collect the money, we had to parade in our street at 9am, be marched to the Winter Gardens and wait for our name to be called. We would then march forward to the pay desk, behind which the paying officer would sit, we would come to attention, salute and collect our pennies. Do a right turn, make our exit and go home for the weekend. This system was adhered to each payday. There were hundreds getting paid and they always used the alphabet starting with A. All the A's would fall in alphabetically, then the B's and so on until they came to 'R S T and all the rest'. How I wished my name had been Anderson. It was usually about 12 noon when I got away to travel to Wigan. We returned to our digs on Sunday night, ready for parade on Monday morning. This was the routine until our final trade test and posting.

AC First Class off to Topcliffe

Chapter 10

102 Squadron Bomber Command, Topcliffe

I passed out as an AC 1st class and was duly posted to 102 Squadron, Bomber Command, Topcliffe, Yorks. There were two squadrons operating from Topcliffe, the other was 77 Squadron which was mainly made up of Canadians and Poles. These squadrons had just been bombed out of Driffield and had been re-equipped with Armstrong Whitworth Whitley bombers. I think they were mark V's. These were fitted with two Rolls Royce Merlin engines and were known as the flying pigs. This was because of their flying attitude, as they appeared to be nose and tail down. Our flight had been modified to accommodate the Merlin engines as the old Bristol Radials did not give sufficient power and therefore altitude. As the bombing runs were done in the company of other types, usually Wellingtons, it was necessary for the old 'flying pigs' to keep up.

This was the winter of 1940/41. And what a winter!

Our aircraft were all parked out on dispersal. That meant that they were parked outside around the perimeter of the field so that if an enemy bomber dropped a stick of bombs, it would probably only take out one aircraft. The hangar would only be used for major servicing. The airfield was just that, no runways like modern airports, just a fairly level field, large enough for heavily laden aircraft to get airborne.

Our work mainly consisted of carrying out the daily inspection, which every flying aircraft gets. The riggers would check the airframe to ensure that all the controls etc. were in good working order. We, the engine mechanics, would check over the engines ensuring that there were no oil or coolant leaks and that everything was secure etc. The armourers would check over the gun turrets and reload the ammunition. There were four Browning machine guns in the rear turret. All operated together and were controlled by a pair of handles which the gunner kept his hands on whilst in operation. The turret was hydraulically controlled and just by moving his hands from left to right and up and down, the whole turret would swing through almost 180 degrees and about 90 degrees up and down. The triggers were in the handles and by just squeezing the handles all four guns would burst into life. Each gun had its own ammunition box and the belts of ammunition were assembled with tracer bullets at intervals so that when they were fired, the tracer bullets would heat up and glow, showing the line of fire. I got to fire a burst when assisting the gunners in the testing. We would require their assistance when we had to run up the engines.

As these aircraft did not have tricycle undercarriages there was a tendency for the tail to lift as the throttles were opened and it was beholden of us to recruit assistance to hang on the tail to keep it down. On a bitterly cold day, it was not an easy job! We would sit in the pilot seat after first making sure that the chocks were properly positioned in front of the main landing wheels, start up the engines one by one, making sure that the control column was held well back. Open them up to about 3,000 revs. Knock off one of the magneto switches and watch the drop in revs. Then switch it back on and switch off the other one, again noting the drop in engine revs. Providing these were within certain limits they would pass OK. When all were satisfied we would adjourn to the flight office to sign up Form F700. No aircraft flew without that form being signed every day!

When operations were on, we would see that the aircraft was full of fuel. (100 octane petrol) The armourers would load them with bombs. Sometimes incendiary, sometimes high explosive and sometimes a mixture of the two, depending on the particular mission. Just before the crew arrived by lorry we would start up the engines and get them up to working temperature before handing the plane over to the crew. There was no heating in these aircraft and the crew needed every bit of warm clothing they could obtain. Once the rear gunner got into his turret in the Whitley, he was there until the plane landed after the op.

During my spell at Topcliffe, we experienced the coldest weather for many, many years. Ops were cancelled. The aircraft were frozen to the turf. We had to erect tents over each engine and light paraffin heaters below to prevent the coolant freezing. This we had to check the specific gravity of by draining a small quantity and bringing it back to the crew room to be checked. I consider that to be the coldest job that I have experienced in my entire life. I was wearing woollen mittens but had to have the fingers exposed in order to be able to use a spanner. These were so cold that one felt that one's fingers were going to stick to it.

Once the frost thawed and we managed to get the engines running again, it was decided to give one a test flight. I volunteered to go up with it and the pilot let me stand behind his seat for a trip out over the North Sea. We were only aloft for about 20 minutes or so but it was long enough for me to realise what an operation would be like!!

My allotted accommodation at Topcliffe was in the ground floor dining room of a house in married quarters, which would have been occupied by a family in peace time. There was little or no heat as the only fuel on the unit was coke and it was most difficult to get hold of. In the next bed to me was a rather rotund character who's name I can no longer remember but his pre-war job was travelling for Cross and Blackwell selling tinned food. There were a number of us using this house as a billet and I have no idea who was actually responsible for it. However, one morning as we awoke from our frozen slumbers it was to see our boots floating by the bed, along with everything else which was on the floor, saturated. It appeared that there had been a burst in the loft and as the thaw set in the water had been cascading down all night.

It was on one morning about this time that I fell foul of a jumped up snivelling little pilot officer. I had been out early to the aircraft and was walking back to the mess for breakfast when I failed to give him a salute. It would appear that they had been told to tighten up on discipline. "Airman" he said, "Why did you not salute me?" I replied that I had been sort of daydreaming and failed to see him. "Did you shave this morning?" "No Sir." I replied. "Number rank and name?" He said, "You are on a charge." I subsequently appeared before the C.O. and got seven days confined to barracks.

Being confined to camp, as it was known did not consist of just not being allowed out. Oh no! We were required to parade in full kit, outside the Guardroom at 1800 hours. This meant, great coat, backpack, and full webbing including water bottle, (full of water) as I was to learn the hard way! Brasses polished, boots shining and hair neatly trimmed. A Sergeant in the RAF Police (Red Cap) took the parade. There would be about ten of us. Everything was done at the double. This meant we had to run up and down whilst the NCO would amble along calling out the time, Left, Right, Left, Right. When we got too far ahead of him, he would shout, "Mark Time!" There we would be, running on the spot whilst he caught up with us, then he'd shout, "Forward!" Then off we would go again. Just when we were about in a state of collapse, we got the command, "Halt!" This was not the end of our jankers as it was known. We were then marched, at the double to the Administration Block where we were given certain duties to perform. I got the Orderly Room floor to polish. All the offices were covered in thick brown linoleum. The system was to spread dollops of yellow/brown wax polish around the floor. This would be spread around with a cloth underneath a tool known as a 'bumper'. When it was nice and dull and evenly spread, a polisher would be put under the bumper and the thing would be pushed backwards and forwards until the floor shone like glass. That bumper must have weighed half a hundred weight, and I must have lost half a stone as I was still wearing great coat and full pack. Needless to say, I caught the flu, reported sick and was put on light duties. (Got out of that one!)

Getting out of camp was no big deal at Topcliffe. The nearest town was Thirsk, which had a market place, a café and a couple of pubs as far as I recall. Went there a couple of times but found more entertainment in the NAAFI. (Navy, Army and Airforce Institute.) There was one on every unit in the RAF. It was a sort of shop where one could purchase the necessities of life. There were usually tables and chairs at the front of the bar where one could augment the RAF ration with beans on toast etc. and what ever else was going at the time. I must say that we fared better than the civilian population when it came to food rationing. I remember one particular air raid that took place about 6pm when we were in the mess having our evening meal. We had pilchards on the plate, the sirens sounded and we had to leave everything and dash for the shelters. Sometime later, after the 'all clear' we returned to the mess to find quite a number of well-fed cats rambling about the tables.

The engine note of German bombers, which at that time were able to reach the far corners of England, had a peculiar pulsating sound. One would hear them flying over with a wow, wow, wow note and hope that it was going to pass without dropping anything. After the Driffield bombing and during my time with the squadron we were subjected to casual raids, which appeared almost as if a lone aircraft couldn't find their target and decided to shoot up our airfield, usually, without any warning. It was then a mad scramble for any protection one could find. On one occasion, I was walking back from the aircraft, which was out on dispersal, when I heard the sound of machine gun fire. It was a lone German bomber, evidently without any bombs so he decided to shoot up the airfield before returning home. Fortunately I was quite close to an anti-aircraft gun emplacement. This was a sort of pit, surrounded by sandbags, where the gun crew manned an ack-ack gun. I cleared those sandbags, I believe head first so they told me afterwards.

My days at Topcliffe came to a close after a few months and I received a posting to Cosford Camp, which was another training unit where the RAF apprentices were trained in peacetime. Here, I underwent a course to upgrade my technical qualification to that of a Fitter 11E. This was a Group 1 tradesman and put me on the top rates of pay for which I was very grateful!!

Chapter 11

Cosford/Stafford/Hoylake

Cosford Camp, being a pre-war establishment, had permanent accommodation blocks and I was allocated a bed in a room in one of the barrack blocks. This room had about 12 beds down either side. The guy in the next bed to me was a wily little Londoner who's name I cannot recall. He was up to all sorts of tricks. He would make extra cash by offering to iron shirts, press slacks etc. and was always running raffles for his own benefit. He would dodge out of camp without a pass by stealing a ride in the back of an ambulance which left camp every morning to go to the local Military Hospital. He would then hitch a ride into London. How he got back into camp I have no idea but he was never on a charge as far as I knew.

I was to come across him later when sitting in the Services Club, in Johannesburg, South Africa whilst watching a show. I was sitting in my seat when I felt a stick prodding into my back. When I looked around, there he was, dressed in the uniform of a South African Airforce Private, complete with swagger cane. It appears that the Draft that he was in was on its way to the Middle East and he didn't fancy that, so he jumped ship at Cape Town and joined the South African Air Force as a welder, doubling his pay in the bargain!

He also had another enterprise. The service issue uniform trousers were rather narrow in the leg and the preferred fashion was to have them a bit wider. If we could supply him with a tunic belt he could have his mate insert the material into the inner seam of each leg in the shape of an elongated V, repress them and it made a really smart job. I can't remember how much he charged but you can bet that he made on the deal. I had a pair done and they became my No.1 pair.

On passing out from Cosford as a Group Engine Fitter, I was posted to No.16 Maintenance Unit at Stafford. This was a huge unit, consisting of six sites. I was employed on No. 6 Site, which was a large storage depot where I was involved in preparing engines for sea travel to protect them from corrosion and packing them in crates. I also got involved in making engine slings by splicing eyelets into wire cables as each engine had its own lifting gear. I think that many of us were sort of 'marking time' until our draft came up for an overseas posting.

As we were all trained in the use of firearms, we were occasionally used for guard duty. This usually consisted of sleeping in the Guardroom, drawing a Lee-Enfield 303 rifle and five rounds of ammunition and standing guard for a couple of hours on whatever needed protecting. Then standing down for a couple of hours whilst someone else took over. This went on all night and provided there were no problems it was work as usual the following day. We were also detailed for fire watching duties on a roster system. Along with others, I was detailed for No.6 Site. There were about half a dozen beds in one of the workshops and we would sleep there until an air-raid warning went off. We would then make our way to the roof of the building complete with a stirrup pump and buckets of water. There were always buckets of sand kept on the roof. Fortunately, I was never called upon to use any of it, as there were no incendiary or indeed any other sort of bomb dropped in our vicinity during my watches. The stirrup pump was a simple pump, which one stood in a bucket of water. Alongside and attached to the pump, was a bracket which was outside the bucket, the base of which had a flat disc with which one held the pump in position by placing one's foot on it. The pump was then operated by a twin-handled grip. It was of the double acting type so water was propelled from the nozzle by both pulling the handle up and by pushing it down. Some of these are still around today and were very popular during the War as this simple device saved many, many buildings. It could cope quite adequately with an ordinary incendiary bomb.

16 MU also appeared to be an assembly unit for gathering together drafts for overseas postings. I was not there long before I was informed that I was included in No. 254 Draft. (I think that was the number) The drill then was to report at the stores for kitting out. This consisted of Tropical Kit, long khaki shorts and tunic, extra kit bag, pith helmet, ground sheet, which was a sort of waterproof cape, and a blanket. We then had to await further instructions. Of course, we had no idea where we were going as secrecy was of paramount importance in war time as the enemy at that time was having great success in sinking our ships and it was in our own interest not to talk about any troop movements.

The draft was eventually brought together and we were transferred to a holding sight at Hoylake on the Wirral. This was a tented camp and we were billeted six to a tent. These were bell tents with a centre pole and we slept on palliasses, a bag full of straw, with our feet to the centre. Enquiries among the other members of the draft revealed that we were a motley crew of many trades and we felt we were being sent to 'restock' some overseas unit, which had become depleted of certain personnel.

Hoylake is just on the other side of the Mersey from Liverpool. At this time, late July/early August 1941, Liverpool was suffering regular nightly air raids. The anti-aircraft batteries surrounding the city were extremely active. All the shells that they sent aloft had to fall somewhere and a great number fell on Hoylake, at least on our camp. Some tents were damaged and I believe there were a few injured airmen. We used our kit bags over our heads to get some protection. The daytime was fine. The weather was lovely. We were confined to camp as we were told that we had to be ready to move at a moment's notice. However, I managed to get a message to my then girlfriend and she paid me a visit before I left. There was a back gate to the camp which I managed to slip out of whilst my mates covered for me. We said our 'good byes', she departed for her home in Great Harwood and I returned to the tent for another couple of days.

Early one morning we were told to pack our gear. Items which were not required on the voyage were to be put in the kit bag with the two blue stripes around it as this would be going in the hold of the ship and our pack and the other kit bag we were to keep in our possession. The pack issued to the RAF consisted of two webbing bags, held together by webbing straps that were held on our backs by straps over the shoulders attached to the webbing waist belt. The upper and smaller of the two packs contained a change of clothing and our small kit (toothbrush, shaving kit etc.) the lower pack contained our great coats. The blanket was rolled in the ground sheet and fastened around the backpack. We were marched to the station carrying full pack and two full kit bags, where we entrained for Liverpool.

Chapter 12

Reina del Pacifico

"Reina del Pacifico"

Awaiting us at the Liverpool docks was a troop ship, The Reina del Pacifico. (Queen of the Pacific I believe!) We were marched aboard and as we got to the top of the gangplank a crew member stuck a ticket between our teeth and directed us either forward or aft. As we filed along another member of the crew directed us to the mess-deck indicated on our tickets. Mine was on the starboard side, just forward of amidships. This mess-deck consisted of about ten tables, covered in brown linoleum, with a bench on either side, which would accommodate eight men, (i.e. sixteen men to a table.) Above the table, fixed into the roof supports, was a series of large hooks. The room was hot as there was little ventilation whilst in port and there were a number of flies about. My first impression was that the ship had been transporting beef from the Argentine and these hooks were where it had been hung. However, I was soon to realise that the hooks were there to sling our hammocks for sleeping. This was to be quite an experience! Not just sleeping in a hammock, which I later got quite comfortable in, but the way we were jammed up against one another.

The system for dining was for the two airmen at the outer end of the table to act as orderlies. They were detailed to go to the galley for the food and to return the empty plates etc. We all moved down the table to take our turn. I don't know how many mess-decks there were but there were 3,500 troops aboard. Officers and female nurses (there were about a dozen nurses on board) had a certain area of one deck out of bounds to other ranks.

The ship stayed in Liverpool for a day or so then weighed anchor and we pulled out into the Mersey. On leaving the Mersey the ship sailed North and we awoke one morning to find ourselves anchored in the River Clyde just off Greenock. There were other ships around and we were here to assemble the convoy, which would be escorted by ships of the Royal Navy.

After about 36 hours we set sail, along with a number of other ships of all sorts of shapes and sizes. Some were troop ships, others were small cargo ships and we headed North for some time before turning West. All the time zig zagging all over the b..... Atlantic.

During my young and formative years, I have suffered from an extremely delicate stomach. I have never been able to travel in the back of a car without being travel sick and where ever possible I prefer to drive. I have been known to feel sick on the Isle of Wight ferry so one can imagine how I was feeling after a couple of days at sea in the North Atlantic. The rest of the members of my mess table fed very well in that first week. I now suffer from a hiatus hernia, which I am convinced is a result of the three days that I spent getting my 'sea legs' as they say. Not only was I continually sick but I had diarrhea as well. At this point, perhaps I should explain the layout of the latrine. Our nearest one was on the port side, running across towards amidships, and consisted of a step up to a series of about eight stalls, without doors, which had wooden boards running the length of the latrine with a hole in each stall. Beneath this was a trough, again running the whole length of all the stalls, which contained water. I presume that it discharged into the sea as the water flowed backwards and forwards with the roll of the ship. The outer stall soon became my favourite as the boards stopped short of the end, leaving a gap down which I could also be sick. Some time after recovering from my seasickness, which lasted for about three days, I was using a stall when there became much consternation from all the users at that time. Someone decided to play a practical joke and put paper down one of the holes and set fire to it. As the ship rolled the paper floated along beneath us. There was a lot of shouting. Then before the paper burned out, it returned as the ship rolled the other way. We never discovered the culprit but we had a good idea who was responsible. No one would go to the toilet with him again.

At least two cruisers and a number of destroyers escorted the convoy. Because of the number of ships and the distance apart we were never able to see the whole of it, we were just interested in the vessels in our immediate vicinity. These were just small tramp steamers and were only capable of travelling at a few knots so we had to travel at the speed of the slowest.

There was some enemy activity whilst we were in the convoy. There must have been a submarine about as there was much naval activity on one occasion after we had been at sea for about a week. The cruiser just off our port bow suddenly went missing. Then a destroyer came down the convoy at full speed. That was a sight I'll never forget. It seemed so fast as we were sailing in the opposite direction. The bow seemed to be rising out of the water. When some distance behind, it began firing off depth charges. By this time I had gone below decks and did they rattle the plates of our ship. I thought the old Reina was going to pop her rivets.

Once over the sickness, I began to enjoy the voyage, especially when we got into the warmer weather and we were able to sleep on deck. The only problem with that was the early rising before the crew came to swab the decks. We spent most of our time either reading or playing 'housey' as we knew it, commonly known as bingo. We did have some PT parades but they were few.

The crew also ran a shop where we could obtain general supplies at extortionate prices. After we had been at sea for about a month and must have been well down Africa, suddenly oranges appeared in the shop. This was August 1941 and we had not seen oranges for a couple of years. We would have paid any price they asked. However, there was trouble brewing for these greedy sailors as the oranges had obviously been purchased on their previous trip and kept in deep freeze. When they were peeled, the centres were all black. There was nearly a riot on board! This shop appeared to be a perk of the catering staff.

We had a ceremony when crossing the Equator for the first time, as most of us were. Someone dressed up as Father Neptune and there was much splashing of water and hose pipes being turned on everyone. A good soaking was had by all. This all happened on my 21st Birthday. That evening, three of my mates and myself went down to the crew's bar and spent the evening playing cards and drinking bottled Bass. That was another crafty scam they had. At the start of the evening the guy behind the bar brought out a baby's enamel bath with a huge block of ice in it. He then proceeded to take the tops off four bottles of Bass at a time and pour them over the ice until the bath was full. It was great at first drinking nice cold beer but as the night wore on and we became more inebriated, the ice was melting and the beer was getting weaker. It wasn't until the following morning that we realised that we had paid the price of beer for that block of ice. We were captive customers as there was nowhere else to spend our money.

Fresh water was rationed practically from the outset. It would only come on for a certain length of time during the day and as the only storage vessel we possessed was our pint drinking mug, it was a case of what shall I do with it? Drink it? Shave in it? Or rinse my hair? I'm afraid I used it for all three from time to time. There were showers aboard but they only delivered seawater and we had to purchase seawater soap. I don't know what it was made of but it was useless for washing anything.

After about three weeks at sea, the convoy was splitting up all the time as we sailed South and we awoke one morning with land in the distance. It turned out to be Freetown in Sierra Leone. We sailed into the harbour and anchored. There were two other troop ships also anchored in the bay where we were to take on fresh supplies and water. As soon as the anchor went down a host of small 'bum boats' came out to greet us. These were pukka dug out canoes, some crewed by small children who would be selling fruit, bananas, mangoes, limes, etc. We would drop a line over the side and haul their baskets up, putting the agreed money in and lowering it. The skill with which they were able to balance and manoeuvre these craft with a single paddle, operated by someone sitting in the stern was amazing. They would also beg for us to throw coins down when one of them would jump in the water and swim down for it before it sank too deep. Some would have a child in the boat and they would shout, "Pickanin dive Glasgow Tanner." Sometimes the Pickanin would dive for them and come up with it in his mouth. Other times the adult would go for it. All the time troops would wrap coppers in silver paper, hence the term, 'Glasgow Tanner'.

No one was allowed ashore and after about three days we left to sail South again. The convoy was now non-existent as far as we were concerned. A cruiser would occasionally put in an appearance. It was named after a city, I think it was Glasgow. The weather was really hot and most of the time we spent on the deck watching the flying fish and dolphins accompanying us. At night, it was total darkness. There were no lights showing on the ship but it was surrounded by a florescent glow as it cut through the water. There was moonlight of course but I was amazed at the number of stars that were visible to the naked eye.

The trip became quite enjoyable from then on. We had no idea where we were going or what lay ahead so I guess we were just living for the moment. Five weeks and four days after leaving Liverpool, land appeared on the horizon in the form of Table Mountain and we subsequently docked in Capetown, South Africa. Our draft was ordered to get our kit together and disembark. A couple of other drafts also left the ship. The trains that were awaiting us at the docks were soon loaded and we pulled out of Capetown docks just as it was getting dark.

Chapter 13

Potchefstroom

The South African trains in 1941 were powered by steam locomotives and were much longer than trains in the UK. They were of a narrower gauge and we soon realised why as we wound our way through the Great Karoo. Even so, some of the bends caused the wheels to screech against the rails. The carriages had corridors and each compartment would sleep six. A top bunk pulled down, the back of the seat lifted up and the seat became the third bunk. They all seemed to be upholstered in green leather. This was a time of strict apartheid. The train was white only but the majority of the train crews were mixed race. This was one of the few places where they could find employment, as they were not made welcome in either the white or black communities. We had been previously warned about the colour bar that operated in South Africa and warned that any fraternisation would result in a five-year jail term. Despite this, we were much more familiar with the Africans than the locals and certainly benefited from their co-operation at times. This colour bar took quite a lot of 'getting used to' for us as the vast majority of us came from a normal working class or at least middle class background. There was a considerable amount of opposition to South Africa's support for the Allies during the war as a large proportion of the white population were of German extraction. I believe that it was only by a couple of votes in their parliament that they entered the war.

Each train had a dining car and we were introduced to some unusual food for us, such as pumpkin as a vegetable and rice instead of potatoes. All was beautifully prepared on board the train and served by the waiters with amazing skill as the train was always rocking from side to side and they would carry plates of food all the way up their arms without anything falling off. There was no such thing as a microwave oven so everything had to be cooked in the train's galley.

After leaving Cape Town, I can still remember the train weaving its way through the Great Karoo Mountains with an extra engine up front. This was dispensed with the following morning as the terrain was flat veldt for miles and miles. Information began to circulate that our draft was to set up an Elementary Flying Training School at Kroonstad but, as it was not yet ready for occupation, we were to detrain at Potchefstroom in The Orange Free State.

We arrived at Potchefstroom, which appeared to be a South African Air Force recruiting unit, and were allocated tents, a palliasse and an area to erect our tents. The area was suffering a number of months of drought conditions. The ground was mainly baked sand, almost red in colour and rock hard. It was virtually impossible to get a tent peg in more than about two inches. However, once home was established we set off to find the NAFFI to top up on the cookhouse grub. There was a film in progress when we arrived. I have no idea what it was but we had only just sat down when there was an almighty roar from the audience and the loudest noise I'd heard for some time. It appeared that the drought had suddenly ended. The loud noise was caused by large hailstones hitting the corrugated iron roof and the South Africans going wild and running outside to run around in it. You can imagine what we thought, coming from rainy old Britain. I'm afraid this little story doesn't end there! On arriving back at the tent that was, there was just a heap of wet gear. Some thoughtful campers had dug a trench around the eaves of their tent and were holding on to their belongings which were reasonably dry.

Potchefstroom was a University town, with many students who disagreed with South Africa entering the war. As a result, conflict built up against any service personnel including newly arrived members of the RAF. During the short while that I was there, one member of the South African Air Force was assaulted one night. They placed his legs over the kerb and ran over them with a car. We took great care when leaving camp after that!

On this camp, there was an enclosed compound which was a detention and correction centre for convicted black Africans. We would see them marched out of the compound in the heat of the day, by their white guards, at the double, each carrying a huge boulder. At the end of the session we marvelled at their fitness as they began throwing these boulders about. Another amazing feature of their background was their skill with pick and shovel. Many of them were ex gold miners, recruited in their bush homelands and transported down to Johannesburg to work deep underground. Most were completely uneducated and were taught all they needed to know for extracting the valuable ore. The powers that be, decided that a trench needed to be dug alongside one of the roads in the camp and a detail was brought out of the compound to carry this out. A line of about ten black men, stripped to the waist, lined up in the appropriate spot and at a command from one of them they all lifted their pick axe in unison. All the picks came down together to a rhythmical chant and this continued as the channel progressed. As the picks were raised, they would spin them around and around, still singing, then down they would come in perfect unison again. It was quite entertaining to watch. The white guard just stood there twirling his sjambok (a whip made of rhinoceros hide). I was told that the reason for all this was so that they would all do the same amount of work. May be it was true?

Some tradesmen, namely storekeepers, were given jobs in the camp stores and they got allocated a bed in one of the huts. Anyone who had a job on the camp got to sleep in a proper bed in a hut. My No.1 mate at the time was a chap called Eric Fellows, a storekeeper with a bed and knowledge of a spare bed which I was to occupy as a, self appointed, controller of the men who kept the boilers fired up so that there was plenty of hot water for the showers. It worked! I was challenged once and my explanation seemed to hold up as I remained in that billet until I, along with three other RAF Fitters, was posted to Wanderboom in the Transvaal where we were to become instructors, attached to the South African Air Force School of Technical Training.

995725 Sanderson I/c hot water and mate

November 1941

Chapter 14

Wanderboom

Wanderboom, as well as being a school of technical training, was also a flying training school equipped with Tiger Moths. It is situated about 5 or 6 miles North of Pretoria in the Transvaal and some 30 to 35 miles North of Johannesburg.

My time at the training school seemed very boring. Most of the time was spent with a Gipsy Major engine attached to a steel stand, which could be inverted and a wooden stand which would take all the disassembled bits and pieces. I would get groups of students for a few days and we would strip the engine down, teaching them the names of the various parts, before reassembling it. They would move on and I would get another group and we would start all over again. After a few weeks, I only had to whistle and the nuts and bolts of that engine would spin off themselves!

After a couple of months or so, the South African Air Force decided that they would train WAAF's to be Flight Mechanics. Now the scene changes! I would get four or five young women to instruct every few days. That was a very interesting time for me. They appeared to be fascinated by my north country British accent and would have me continually repeating the words 'gudgeon pin', which is the pin that connects the piston to the connecting rod. Someone christened me Corporal Tommy and it stuck! "What's this called Corporal Tommy?" "That's a gudgeon pin Susan!" They delighted in taking the mickey but it was a very interesting time and there were off duty moments when we were not talking engines!

A couple of stripes

We were given a couple of stripes and the rank of acting corporal. The South Africans were full sergeants. Unfortunately we didn't get the rise in pay and it took a lot of pressure from us to get the rank substantiated as we were unable to get a RAF trade test out there, which was essential to first get upgraded to Leading Aircraftman before promotion. However, we finally succeeded and got the pay that we rightly deserved.

For the majority of our leave and weekend passes we caught the train to Johannesburg where there was a Services club which had accommodation of sorts. The members of the public who were disposed to laying on treats for the service personnel would leave messages at the club, such as, 'Two Boys To Attend A Dance. Will Be Collected At 7PM.' At the

Post Office savings book

time I was accompanied by a RAF mate from the school, Jock McGurin. He was a rigger and was instructing on airframes. We put our names on the list and were duly met by two gorgeous girls, the Weinan sisters. We introduced ourselves and I accompanied Joy. She informed me that she had a car but it was parked out of town as she had only just started driving. "Do you drive?" She asked. We caught the bus out of town and picked up her car which was an American Hudson Terraplane with a rear dickey seat. She had just bought it, second hand, and the salesman had told her that if the engine failed to run, she was to pour water over, what she pointed out, was the distributor. She carried a bottle of water in the car for this purpose. On this occasion, we had no trouble but I later found out what it was all about. Jock and Joy's sister got into the dickey seat and I drove her car back to her home in Parktown North (a suburb of

Jo'burg) where the girls got changed and we all went off for the evening.

Joy's father had died some nine or ten years before we met. He was a haemophiliac and died from having a tooth out. It appears that this condition applies to males and the gene is carried by the female so there was every chance that her offspring could be affected. I was always conscious of this and made sure that I was not going to be husband material as many of the South African girls were looking for Europeans. (Northern Europeans at this time were practically an all white population, and apartheid in South Africa was at its height.) Our relationship continued for some time. On one occasion, whilst we were out for a picnic in the Hudson, the engine stopped. She duly got out her bottle of water and was about to pour it over the distributor when I stopped her as I suggested that perhaps she had made a mistake as to where the water should be poured. There would be no chance of the engine starting again with the electrics all wet. We sat there for some time, the engine cooled down and it started up again and ran fine all the way home. The trouble was vaporisation in the fuel pump and fuel pipe to the carburettor. Being the great engineer, I said, "I'll fix that for you." She said, "I don't need it. Take it back to camp with you and I'll see you next weekend." So come Sunday night, I drove it back to Wanderboom and had the car for a week. I spent a couple of hours making a scoop to deflect air from the cooling fan on to the vital parts, attached it to the fuel pump and we had no more bother. We had a great time with Joy and her family. Her mother had married again and she had a half brother who was about 8 or 9 and completely 'spoiled'. During my time with the Fourie family as they were then called, I was still engaged to the 'girl back home' and so did not stray completely from 'the straight and narrow'. A fact of which I am quite proud despite the enormous temptation. She had a model figure, was almost as tall as me, and was a cracking dancer. We were frequent visitors to the Wanderers Club in Johannesburg, which was the rugby club of Jo'burg and had a huge dance floor. Writing this has brought back so many happy memories!

The Fourie/Weinan Family taken by Joy

Chapter 15

In the Bush

Another family I met as a result of a contact from the Services Club was a man called Cam. I have forgotten his second name. He was a director of the Whitwater Rand Water Board. He and his wife invited my mate and me to stay the weekend with them on several occasions. They had no children. He was an excellent cook and we had some super Sunday lunches with them. We earned our keep by concreting some slabs down his front drive. I expect my name is still there in one of those concrete slabs. Cam had a friend who lived up country on the borders of what was then Southern Rhodesia. He lived with his wife in a native constructed thatch bungalow, very open plan to allow the breeze to pass through. He had a business, transporting African mine workers from a camp about 100 miles further up north, down to his base where they could walk the ten miles or so to the nearest railway station at what I believe was Soekmekaar. For transport, he was using Ford Trucks with the famous Ford V8 engines and it so happened that he didn't have a worker to fit the big end bearings of one that he was having overhauled. "Would you two like a couple of weeks holiday in the bush in return for a little work on the engine?" So, arrangements were made, we both got a couple of weeks leave and off we went North to the station at Soekmekaar where we were met by our host (who's name I have forgotten) in his truck and driven about 10 miles North across the dried up bed of the Limpopo River to his home.

Cam's friend's bungalow

We were made very welcome. He was originally from England but had lived most of his 50 years or so in Africa. He never left home without his Lee-Enfield .303 rifle and he also carried a smaller .22 rifle. Just before dusk on the day of our arrival he took us out to find something for breakfast. He could see things in the bush that were invisible to us and it was not long before he spotted a duiker (a small deer). After he pointed it out to us we were still unable to see it. Mind you, he knew what he was looking for and we were a pair of really 'green' hunters. However, he brought up his rifle and it was despatched with a single shot. We had deer's liver for breakfast the following morning. It was delicious!! Breakfast over and a couple of hours in his workshop hut and the engine was well on its way to being rebuilt which was left to his African workers. The next thing was to go out hunting for the Pot!

Hunting

Jock, myself and the guy we were staying with (I wish I could remember his name), set off in his utility vehicle and soon came across a water buffalo which had sustained a rather large wound. We very gingerly alighted from the vehicle and I was given the dubious honour of despatching it with the 303 rifle. I was instructed where to aim the bullet and it seemed to work first time but I gave it a second round just in case. We didn't take it back but it was given to the Africans who would have eaten it. I reckon it would have been a bit tough for us.

They had electric light which came on when they started the engine and generator. There was a shower room which was of the usual wooden frame with thatch and an open top with a frame which held a container. When one wanted a shower, the container would be filled with water and by pulling a cord, the water would cascade down. Most efficient! The door to the shower will remain in my memory as one had to negotiate a hornet's nest to get in and were they big things! At sundown, a delightful time in Africa, the brandy bottle would be produced. Everybody had a little tipple before dinner just to be sociable. The sun sets really quickly out there and it is a signal for the 'dive bombers' to become active. It took some getting used to the flying insects which appeared at sundown. Not just the quantity, but the size of them. They would be banging themselves against the lights all night, and the noise of the crickets was incessant. One soon got used to that as it was fairly constant throughout Africa.

It so happened that our host had a truck load of mine workers returning to their homelands having been working in the Johannesburg gold mines, for usually a three year stint. He evidently had two loads to come from his other camp which was about 80 to 100 miles North so he asked me if I would drive the empty truck up for him. He drove the full one together with his wife and I took the other with Jock McGurin riding 'shotgun'. They loaded themselves into the one truck, together with all the possessions that they had acquired, including cycles which were piled on top. (I'm just thinking of our health and safety laws). We were given a couple of 303 rifles and directed to follow them. There were no roads, just two wheel tracks through the bush. These became quite rough in places where tree roots crossed. I had my rifle under my legs alongside the front of the seat but Jock had put his on the seat beside him and on one bump, as he leapt into the air, he came down on the butt of his rifle and broke it in two pieces. The remainder of the journey was uneventful as I remember until we arrived at the Northern Camp. This was a time of the year when the rivers were dried out into waterholes. Some were quite large like lakes as the rivers were often hundreds of yards wide. The point where we crossed the Limpopo must have been half a mile wide as we were able to see hippos basking in the pool. If fact, our host picked up his .22 and shot at one of them. There's no doubt that he hit it but it never flinched.

The Northern Camp was similar to the main camp in construction but was not far from a large waterhole which we were able to watch in the evening as various types of animals came down to bathe and drink, a herd of elephants on one occasion. We stayed there for a couple of days whilst the passengers gathered, then set off one morning with two loads of men from the remote areas of Southern Rhodesia as it was then. They had nothing but what they stood up in. My knowledge of their Bantu language being non-existent, we communicated by sign language and got along fine. A sense of humour is universal!

The journey back South was a little smoother as the weight of the load steadied the old truck, fortunately for the passengers. I have no idea what they paid for the trip but luxury travel it certainly was not! We had been travelling for a couple of hours when we had a puncture in the rear offside tyre. As we were 'following my leader', the others were unaware of our problem. Unfortunately, I was unable to find a jack but found a wheel brace so was able to loosen the wheel nuts. We had a spare wheel so all that was required was a few strong men to lift the rear offside of the truck and prop it up while I made the change. Well, I had a truck full and with a bit of demonstrating and grunting they got the message and made light work of lifting it while we got a block of wood under it. After making the change, the rest of the trip was uneventful. It was a super holiday and remains, quite vividly, in my memory as one of the most unusual and special two weeks of my African sojourn.

Chapter 16

Kroonstad

My attachment to the Wanderboom School of Technical Training was drawing to a close. We had been there about 14 months and the South African Air Force staff had increased. The four of us made representations to people in charge and we eventually got our Corporal's rank substantiated and therefore got paid! The next thing was to get a posting back to the original No.7 Air School at Kroonstad where we should have gone in the first place.

Before leaving Wanderboom, I had received a letter from home informing me that the girl I was engaged to, was having an affair with a married man and that some friends of my mother had seen her leaving the sand hills at Blackpool with him. This was my 'Dear John' letter as they were called. There was some correspondence between us and I remember telling her that it was all over and she could flog the ring. Long after returning home, I found out how my mother came by that information. The silly girl left her handbag downstairs whilst staying at our house and as I had not written home for some time, one of the family looked in the bag to see if there was any news and found more than they bargained for. This must have been early 1942 and as I didn't leave South Africa until January 1945, I appreciated the freedom!

In the Air Force, when one gets a posting, the procedure is to report at the Orderly Room, get a Posting Form, then proceed to every department on the unit to get it signed to show that everything that one has borrowed has been returned and that no-one has any reason to require your presence any more. This used to include even the cookhouse. I guess they wanted to make sure that you were not making off with a side of beef or something. On arriving at the new station, one reported to the Orderly Room, got a similar Form and went round all departments to book in. When I left Bomber Command the aircraft consisted of mainly twin engined bombers but we had heard that we were to be equipped with new four engined Halifax Aircraft. It was whilst in the Orderly Room at Kroonstad, booking in, that I saw a memo from the UK asking for engine fitters to volunteer for training as Flight Engineers. It appeared the bigger bombers had to carry an extra crew member to monitor all the engine instruments, attend to the mixture controls etc. and keep the aircraft balance by monitoring the fuel tank contents etc. I thought, I'll get a trip home for training and so volunteered. The next morning, I was sent for by the C.O. He was very nice, but turned me down as he said that I was needed where I was and that the war would be over before I could be returned home and trained. I then reported to the Engineer Officer who gave me a job of assembling a new TigerMoth which had just arrived in crates.

Kroonstad Servicing Hangar

After that I was put in the Servicing Hangar I/c a team keeping the Tigers in the air. It was here that I met up with an old mate that I was originally on the draft with in Stafford, one Eric Fellows. He was also a Corporal, but a 'store basher' i.e. he worked in the stores where spares for the aircraft and tools for the mechanics were stored. In today's vocabulary, 'we hung out together' for several trips into Johannesburg where he had got himself involved with a married woman. Therein lies another story!

One of my duties at this time was supervising the laying out and maintenance of the flare path for the pupils to experience night flying. This consisted of collecting a load of paraffin flares, known as 'Money Flares', which contained 3 or 4 pints of paraffin, with a wick about 2" to 3" thick, sticking out of a spout about a foot long. These were positioned in the shape of a large letter T, spaced out about 10 yards apart, with the head of the T into the wind. The flares were lit, making sure that the wind was blowing the flame away from the paraffin container. The pupils would practice taking off and landing in the dark just with the use of the flare path. Unfortunately I never got to get airborne to see it from above as we only got to fly on the odd test flight and that was always during daylight.

Another duty which came around occasionally was Orderly Corporal. This consisted of accompanying the Orderly Officer on his rounds during the night. After work for the day and if there was no night flying, all the aircraft would be returned to the hangars which were located in a compound, surrounded by a wire fence, with a couple of gates in it. This was patrolled by Black African troops and they also did sentry duty at the gates. At this time in South Africa, sentry duty was carried out with a steel tipped spear, known as an assegai. As we use the rifle for drill purposes, they use the assegai. They did all the usual things like, Present Arms, Order Arms, Slope Arms etc. and they all seemed to love the military life. They were smart and well disciplined. If they were given an order, they carried it out as ordered.

Each night we were given a password which had to be used when entering the restricted area. On this particular night, I was accompanying a 'sprog' officer, full of his own importance and we entered the compound, giving the sentry the password when approached with the command, "HALT, WHO GOES THERE?" I replied, "Orderly Officer." and gave the password. The gate was opened and we went around the hangers. After conducting our inspection, we returned to the gate at which we had entered and again received the command, "HALT, WHO GOES THERE?" Upon which the 'sprog' begins to walk towards the sentry saying, "No. No. My man. You don't challenge us going out." I said, "Stand still Sir." He continued towards the sentry and received an assegai within about two inches of his throat. By this time I had approached, given the password and we were allowed out. The sentry had been told to challenge anyone approaching the gate and he did just that, 'Sprog' was still shaking as we arrived at the guard room.

The town of Kroonstad in the Orange Free State, was quite a small place. It had a railway station and a cinema but very little else. Our recreation consisted mainly of getting drunk and singing bawdy songs in the Corporals' Club. There was an Officers' Mess, a Sergeants' Mess and we Corporals had a Club. There were a few South African WAAFs on the unit but they had a compound of their own. Our club consisted of a comfortable lounge/club room with a well stocked bar in which we took turns in assisting the barman with menial chores. Drinks were mostly Castle Beer or Chateau Brandy, both products of South Africa. We had many weekend sessions and I learned to cope with the amount of alcohol that I could consume without making a fool of myself! Some weekends were spent in Johannesburg and as I was now a free agent they were most enjoyable.

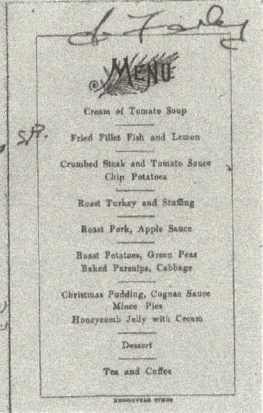

Christmas 1943 Menu

Meanwhile back at home ...

Xmas Evening   22 Gathurst Road

My Dearest Tommy,

Well Xmas day, not dinner time this year but we've just had a tea supper and we're full up once again and lets hope it's the last Xmas that you have a joint letter, George and I have just been talking about the party we shall have when this war is over. We've had plenty to eat goose and pork with all its trimmings, roll on the time when your feet are under the table again. Now I'm passing on to Aunty Flo.

God Bless you Tommy and bring you back safe and sound. Aunty Flo.

Hi Ya Tommy. Looking forward to another feed of fish and chips with you at Common Edge when this shindig is over. All the best. Uncle David.

Well Tom here is the old man after a good day's work but I am at present sober I don't know if Mum is going to mug us after we have written you but I think she will. We drank to you just as Xmas day came in last night with a cocktail made by Dougie at work and it was good. I do hope you have not moved, you are doing what your country requires and they will move you when the time comes so do not bother yourself to get moving again. Well Tom my boy, or should I say man now, Good Luck to you. I wish we could be with you but it won't be long now, the news is good. So stick it and you will be glad after, you are keen I know to get amongst the fighting, but do what the RAF want you to they know best. So again Good Luck Tom and all the best, I will see you have a damn good time when you do come home.

Here's cheers Tommy, be quick and finish the war for us. Joyce

Hallo Tom we're having such a good time all we need is you to play the trumpet. George is playing now, Douglas is learning your part of "Solitude", he played it last Christmas. They're playing it now, it's almost like you playing. Never mind, you never know what next Xmas will bring. Oh I must tell you the dog Monty is hiding from the trumpet he can't stand it at all. You know the little discs we have instead of money when we play Newmarket, well we've just had a "Conga" and I put some in two ashtrays and used them for maracas it was good fun. Well I've not to take too much room. So long Tom we'll be seeing you soon. Love Joan.

Well Tommy, they seem to have told you a lot already so I don't quite know what to add. We've had a lovely weekend but then I always enjoy coming home for it is that to me, a real home. Well Tommy I've never met you but I feel I know you very well, I hear so much about you. I'll have the pleasure of meeting you one day and I hope that day is not too far away so I'll let George add some now. With lots of good luck and all you wish yourself. Mary.

Hiya!

The old and ancient senior brethren speaking. The noise in here is 'orrible - I've just grabbed a break from "knocking it out" and I'm full of food as usual on this piggiest of days.

I wrote to you a few days ago and sent 4 photos of Mary and me, wedding photos of Mary and me and some of us in London. I hope you get them safely. I've been unlucky in that some of my photos have been lost.

I'm just waiting to be taken for a ride - they're playing games and I'm the sucker in chief.

I saw your game hunting letter - you should be a rival to Frank Buck with another year or so out there. I got your cable.

There's nothing more to tell, brother. I guess all there was was in my other letter, so cheers for now and all the best.

Keep it swinging! George.

Hi! Pal, well I ain't boozed up yet but not far off. When you're in the "Wine and Spirit Ale and Stout Merchants" you can't leave Guinness lying about asking to be drunk. Well Pal I expect G has told you about my Special Cocktail, boy some kick. I'll have a bottle for you when you come home. In this cocktail there's Port, Gingerette Liqueur, Brandy, Whiskey, Sherry so you can guess what it tastes like. Douglas (Titch).

Well Tom

I wish old bloody Lord Haw Haw had seen us at dinner today, we would have liked to have starved him for a fortnight and then tied him to the table leg with a ring through his nose and give him a damn good kick up the pants and chucked him in one of the cells. When we get an Air Force boy in Mum always gives him a little bit of something extra. She does love the Air Force because

"Our Tom is in the RAF." Mum is about 3 parts cut, we have just played a game and got her laughing and you know what she's like. Well Tom and any Censor who has the tedious job of censoring letters, all the best to you all. I wish I was in it again but I'm still doing my bit, going away again 8th Jan to the end of the month. It is rotten but as long as we are helping to boot the scum off the seas of the world I don't care. All the best Tom. Dad

Now my Dearest Boy, God bless you and may we soon meet, if the wishes of all are answered from the drinks we had at midnight last night, we shall. All the best Dear, Your Loving Mother, Gran will add her little bit upstairs where she can get the light better.

Here I am Tommy, last of the bunch and not much to add. I hope you received my note and PC safe and I do wish you all the luck in the world and hope you will soon be home with us. The news is certainly good. No more now Ta Ta Gran.

Well my Dear that's the end of the Xmas Party and now everyone has gone and all our good fare gone too, we are down to boiled bacon leeks and potatoes today so it's not quite so appetising I can assure you. We have been promised a goose for New Year so here's hoping, I think I'll ask Grandma over.

Well my Dear I hope you had as good a Xmas as we did and will have all the best for 1944

Fond Love from all and God bless you Tom, your Loving Mother and Dad

xxxxxxxxxxxxxxx

It was soon after arriving at No. 7 Air School that I met up with an airman who played the accordion. He was a parachute packer and was dead keen on forming a dance band. He had gathered together some old instruments which included an old cornet. It was a battered old thing with only one of the three valve tops in place, but it had a mouth piece and a b flat shank which made it just playable as far as I was concerned. "Do you play one of those?" he asked. And I replied that I have been known to knock out the odd tune. "Rehearsal. Tuesday afternoon 3pm. Be there!" And I was. There I met the pianist, clarinet player, drummer and a violinist together with the accordion player. Unfortunately, the names have all gone. I remember that the accordionist was from Bournemouth and the clarinet player was originally from Belgium. When he found out that I could also read music, we were up and running. We started playing for weekly dances in the NAAFI and all was going well. I bought myself a second hand trumpet from a shop in Johannesburg and we really got swinging.

The Band

Our notoriety spread and we were getting engagements in the town. We played for a few bah-mitzvahs and did a turn on the stage at the local cinema. We also provided the music for the wedding of one of our sergeants who married a South African girl.

I'm afraid the trumpet and the rendering of 'Solitude' would often be serenaded to the camp at large when I'd had a session with the lads in the club. The rest of the unit always knew when I'd had a good night!

There is a photograph of me on the same train as the honeymooners somewhere in existence. I was going away for the weekend to a town called Bethlehem, which was just up the line from Kroonstad and I think they were making for Durban.

Train to Bethlehem with the newly weds

I had previously met the Dunbar family who had two daughters, Beryl and the younger daughter who's name escapes me for the moment. They subsequently moved to Cape Town where their grandfather lived and I met up with them again when I moved South to await a boat home. There were a couple of days, when a few of us were bussed out to a naval air station at Simonstown to service some American aircraft that had flown in from an American carrier. I think they were Grumman Hellcats. We never saw the carrier and they flew off back from where they had come. I guess the carrier had been getting short on fuel.

I had some good trips out with the Dunbar family, including a trip up Table Mountain in the cable car. There was also a trip at night, along the coast road going south east from the city centre. I can still remember the lights and the reflections in the sea. I don't know why it should have

Table Mountain with the Dunbar girls

impressed me so much as there had been no black out in South Africa. We spent a good few weeks in Cape Town and most of the days were spent in a bar type lounge, I think it was called The Alhambra. There was a good band playing on the stage every afternoon, and a restaurant balcony where the greatest cray fish salads were served. Delicious!

The invasion of Europe was well under way and things were progressing well according to the news we were getting. We were all looking forward to going home as it had been about three and a half years since we left. Despite this, there was some trepidation among those of us who did not have the security of a job to go back to. What will the future hold? For the past five years or so we had everything found, including food, spending money, a bed to sleep in, all our clothes, and comrades to share a life with. Despite all this we couldn't wait for that boat home.

One morning, our flight was told to pack our gear as our boat had arrived. When we got to the docks, there she was! A Royal Mail Steam Packet liner called The Andes. She had been completed just as war broke out and was immediately returned to the yard and fitted out as a troopship. Our journey home took just over 12 days as opposed to five weeks and four days going out. We were able to travel so fast that the u-boats couldn't catch us, so we were told. But I think the u-boat menace was just about over as it was now January 1945. Living conditions were much better on the Andes and I spent quite a lot of my time helping one of the cooks in our galley.

Cabin 4B RMS Andes

The trip home was quite uneventful as far as I remember. Spent some money playing 'housey' as they called bingo on the ship and duly docked in Liverpool one morning in January 1945. We marched to Lime Street Station to catch a train to Blackpool where we were eventually issued with a three week leave pass and a rail warrant to our home station. My lasting memory of the actual homecoming was the rosy cheeks and fresh faces of the children on Lime Street Station. It was quite surprising how different they looked to what we had become accustomed to.

Chapter 17

Home

I remember travelling to Wigan and leaving some of my mates at the station and catching a bus out to Orrell but things are pretty hazy after that. The last time that I was in Orrell was June, 1941 and here I was back on the same old bus in January 1945. Three and a half years is a long time in a young person's life and 'much water had flowed under the bridge.' I know that there seemed to be a lot of people at home but apart from my mother and father I couldn't swear as to who else was there. It was some welcome! I didn't realise just how much I'd missed everyone.

My mother and father

However, things rapidly got back to normal. Dad was the Inspector I/c the district which covered a fairly large area around Wigan and of necessity had to have a car and therefore petrol coupons. He also knew a friendly farmer known as Freddy Woods. I met Freddy and he was able to lend me a car for a couple of days, together with the coupons to run it. It was used for taking a gang of us dancing at the Blackpool Winter Gardens as well as local runs.

On returning the car, Freddy invited me out for an evening, a drink and a game of darts in a local pub. He didn't tell me that he was meeting his married girlfriend first. When we turned up at her place there were two girls. My partner was a beautiful young, 21 year old, domestic science teacher who was in digs with Freddy's girl friend. This was to be the start of a partnership that was to last for sixty three years to date. I remember getting into the back of the car with her and it was as if we had known one another for years. She wasn't a bad darts player either!

In those days, it was not considered proper for a respectable young teacher to live with a married woman who was having an 'affair' and Cath's Head Master was looking out for some more appropriate accommodation in the village. It so happened that my younger brother Douglas had been called up to do his National Service and my mother offered Cath the chance to come and live with my family in Orrell. It was within travelling distance of her school at Rainford and there was a convenient train service from Orrell Station. This was approved of and Cath came to live with us in about the summer of 1945.

One evening, early on in our 'courtship', we were walking home to Orrell Police Station after dancing the night away at Abbey Lakes dance hall, when I remarked to Cath that I wouldn't mind this continuing for the rest of our days. She replied, "I would rather like that." With that we became engaged much to the delight of my mother who

Cath

in no time at all organised an engagement ring from my Aunty Nelly who was a working jeweller in Manchester.

The first time that I remember Cath taking me to her home in Llangrannog, I can't remember if it was before we became engaged or after, but we travelled down on the train from Wigan to Aberystwyth, changing at Shrewsbury where we caught the 'morning milk train' down to Aberystwyth. It stopped at every little station on the way.

We would meet up whenever I could get leave or a weekend pass. When I was at Jurby in the Isle of Man, there were always planes flying to the mainland and I managed to get a lift on one occasion. I drew a parachute from the stores in Jurby. Nipped on an old Avro Anson (which were used for general transport) and we flew to Valley Anglesey RAF Station in about 20 minutes, where I was able to hand in my parachute and thumb a lift home to Wigan. I was home in about an hour and a half.

My three weeks disembarkation leave was drawing to a close when I received notification of my 'near home' posting. This was to a Maintenance Unit at Wilmslow, south of Manchester. This turned out to be a yard with a row of large garages, an office and loads of equipment and was situated about half a mile down the road from the main RAF Camp where I had originally completed my basic training. It was a Repair on Sight and Salvage Unit. I think we slept at the main camp when we were at the unit. I know that we went up there for our meals as I remember using the same mess as women who had recently been released from the German Concentration Camps. They had shaven heads and tattooed numbers around the tops of their arms. I believe a lot of them were from Poland. This was about February or March 1945. The Allies were moving through Europe and it was obvious that the war was coming to an end. Our job was to clear up the wrecked aircraft which had been left around remote hills and moors after prior removal of the crews.

My first job was to remove three Hurricanes from a remote hillside somewhere outside Tintwistle on the edge of the notorious Saddleworth Moor. It appears that they flew into the hillside in formation. I was I/c with four erks and a Dodge 3 tonner. I had a telephone number to call up a 'Queen Mary' (Commer Artic with a long low loader trailer which would carry a Hurricane mainplane or fuselage in one piece) when we were ready for loading. Arrangements were made for the five of us to sleep at a rifle range which was way out on the Moor. I think it took us about a week to clear the site. What we couldn't manhandle down to the roadway and on to the loader we buried in the hillside. On completion, we returned to our unit and my next job was to draw a toolbox from the store, pack most of my gear and together with another Airman we were issued with travel warrants for Loch Erne in Northern Ireland via Stranraer.

This job was to service the engines of a Sunderland Flying Boat which had been out of service for some months. The hull had been crushed when it was frozen in the ice and had been repaired by Short and Harland of Belfast. On arrival at the Coastal Command Station on Loch Erne we duly reported in to the Guard Room, which is always just inside the main gate at all units, and were allocated sleeping accommodation and shown where to report to the Engineer Officer.

On finding out what was required of us, i.e. to service and get the engines running on a Sunderland Flying Boat which was moored out on the lake, after Tiger Moths, it was quite daunting. However, we didn't rush into it and took our time asking the locals for tips on working on the water. The other man with me had never worked on the water either.

This Sunderland was equipped with four Pratt and Whitney radial engines situated ten or twelve feet above the water. The tools that we had brought with us were almost useless as aircraft engines usually required the use of special tools designed for that particular engine.

(They used to say that the tools for a Rolls Royce Merlin engine cost more than the engine itself.) The tools that we required were drawn from the maintenance store, signed for, and we were warned that we were liable to pay for tools not returned. Lesson No.1, tie everything to one's wrist as dropping a spanner would be a costly business.

Next, we required a launch to get out to the craft. Again we could sign out a boat provided there was one available or we could be transported out and collected later. We managed to get a boat each day and moor it alongside the aircraft. To get to the engines involved getting aboard the flying boat and climbing out of the upper hatch and walking along the mainplane. When I look back now, I can't remember how we managed to remove the cowlings to get to the engines, whether we had platforms which attached to the engine frames or some other cradle system which enabled us to access them, but I know the water was directly under us. As for our tools, they were tied to our wrists with string.

All checks carried out, the next job was to start and run them up. It took some time to work out the controls for starting as neither of us had seen a Sunderland before. However, we found the priming pumps etc. and got one engine running when the pilot and navigator came aboard. After all four were passed OK they announced that we were going for a test flight. I was detailed to take the port drogue, my mate took the starboard one. These were to act as the brakes on landing and steering whilst on the water. The drogues were like canvas buckets with a hole at one end of about two feet in diameter and a hole in the other end of about a foot. They were connected to the fuselage by a rope secured at the larger end so that the forward motion of the craft filled the front end and created drag. It was quite surprising how much drag they developed!

Once we had cast off from the moorings the drogues would not be required until we landed so we were able to stand up with the pilot and enjoy the take off. Some buffeting took place as we gathered speed. It rose onto the 'step' and it got a lot smoother until all went calm as we left the water. We were aloft about ten to fifteen minutes as we circled over Ireland. Then, as we started to descend we, the 'crew', went to our respective drogues to await orders. Once we were down on the lake we opened our respective hatch and duly threw out the 'buckets' when requested. The pilot could steer the flying boat by speeding up the outer engines but the drogues certainly gave him more control. Once the boat was back on its mooring and the engines shut down our job was over.

Whilst returning to my unit I was obliged to spend a night at the RAF camp at Belfast before catching the morning boat to Stranraer. I spent the evening in a picture house in Belfast and it was there that we heard that the war was over in Europe. There was much rejoicing!!!!

It was back to Wilmslow to see where we were going to next.

Chapter 18

Jurby Isle of Man

Clearing up the wreckage

The next 'near home' posting was to Jurby in the Isle of Man. On arrival at Jurby Camp, after a very rough crossing from Liverpool and a bumpy ride in the back of a RAF truck, I found myself I/c four or five erks, in a wooden hut in the corner of the airfield where an old Blenheim Bomber was awaiting dismantling. This was to be a spare time job to keep us occupied when there was nothing more urgent. We spent a considerable time in our hut playing darts during this period and I was getting quite proficient!

One call we had was to recover a Seafire (a SpitFire with clipped wings adapted for use by the Fleet Air Arm) from Ronaldsay, a Fleet Air Arm station on the Island.

The Dodge truck

We arrived in our Dodge truck, pulled up outside the Guardroom just inside the main gate and I went in to report. There was an almighty bellow, "Put that cigarette out on the Quarter Deck!" "Do you mean me?" Oh yes they did. Opposite the Guardroom was an area of grass, which was being mowed by an officer, and the station flag pole looking like it had been blancoed. This apparently was the 'Quarter Deck' which is evidently revered as the place where Lord Nelson fell.

Having duly apologised and put out my fag, we were allocated accommodation in one of the huts where we had double tiered bunks. Not my idea of peaceful sleeping, not for boozy service personnel. However, morning duly arrived and we were awakened by the tannoy loud speaker system, "Wakey! Wakey! Rise and Shine, you've had your time and I've had mine. Hands off cocks and on socks." Followed by other rhymes on occasions. Not at all what we had been used to. Catching the truck to go down to the town in the evening was referred to as 'catching the liberty ship.' Strange these naval types!

The aircraft that we had come for was situated on the far side of the airfield, standing out in the open. Someone had beaten us to it as the clock had been nicked. The tanks were quite full of 100 octane petrol. Our usual procedure was to drain it into containers and hand it over to the motor transport section and get a signature for it as petrol was still a very precious commodity. On enquiring with the engineering department for suitable containers, I met the Engineer Officer who handed me an aircraft clock and said that he had had it removed for safe keeping but it didn't go. As for the containers, he could only supply one 40 gallon drum. "Roll it to the cliff edge and pull the bung out" were his instructions; and so a fair amount of top grade fuel went into the sea. As for the clock - the last I saw of it was when I gave it to my Aunty Nelly (the jeweller) to see if it could be repaired and I forgot all about it for years!! I think it must have gone when she gave up the business!

Close to where this aircraft was parked and on the other side of the perimeter track, was a lonely toilet. No other building around it, just a wooden hut with a toilet in it. I have seen many toilets inscribed with graffiti in my time but nothing to match that little hut. There was not a space for another inscription anywhere in the interior. Among the few I remember such as Kilroy having visited was the following ditty:- You don't come here to sit at ease and rest your elbows on your knees, so sit up straight and you will find, you won't sh.. on the seat behind. No one had taken a blind bit of notice of this one as the toilet appeared to have not been cleaned EVER.

Whilst we were working on this machine, the Fleet Air Arm were experimenting with assisting the take off of an old Fairey Swordfish biplane, with rockets under each wing. It was interesting to see the old kite thrust into the air! It was all a bit late as hostilities were just about to end in the far East, if they had not already ended. It was surprising how the urgency of the job changed after the ending of hostilities. Everything was sort of 'winding down' to await our 'demob'.

Cath was still teaching at Rainford but was able to come across to the Island for the weekend. I got a weekend pass and we spent a very pleasant time, staying at a small hotel/boarding house, in Douglas. Unfortunately, she had a very rough crossing from Liverpool. Even sailors were being seasick so future trips were not going to be very popular.

During my stay in the Isle of Man, I was informed that I had been transferred to a unit somewhere near Shrewsbury I think and that my gear had been moved in my absence. I know that when I eventually caught up with my gear half of it was missing. However, it was just a holding unit where we were to wait for our draft number to travel to Cardington for demobilisation. The hangar where this took place was originally used for building and housing airships. It was huge and made humans seem like midgets.

I received, I think, a couple of weeks' wage, a pinstripe grey suit, a grey trilby hat and a pair of gloves, a shirt and a tie as far as I remember. I think I returned home in my uniform battledress and became a civilian on changing into civvies. How strange this seemed after six years in the same gear and being part of an organisation like the RAF, to be a non-person without a job and nothing to look forward to. I had a lot of adjusting to do but that could all be done after enjoying my demob leave. I found it difficult meeting people at first. I didn't know whether to raise my hat, salute or shake hands.

Chapter 19

Civilian Life

After a couple of weeks leave, I decided to find myself some transport. Despite the fact that petrol was still rationed, I thought my father was getting a bit fed up with my mother persuading him to lend us his car to get about in the evening. They were members of Wigan Repertory Company and we used to borrow their tickets as we could get in for free on a Monday evening.

Cars were scarce and very expensive but I managed to find a little Singer 9 for which I paid, I think, £95. It was trouble with a capital T.

Our first car

I would spend all day working on it so we could go out in the evening. The engine had only three of the four cylinders working. This turned out to be due to the fact that there were no rings on the piston of one cylinder. After stripping it down, I set about the problem of finding spares, which were just about none existent at the end of the war. Whilst wandering around Orrell, I came across a little workshop at the cross roads not far from Orrell Station. There was a considerable amount of rubbish about and among the junk on a windowsill was a packet of piston rings. They look about the right size, I thought! There was no one about. I stayed there for about ten minutes and still no one answered my calls so I returned home complete with packet of rings. They were just about the right diameter but took a considerable amount of rubbing down to get them to fit in the grooves. They worked, and the engine managed to produce sufficient power to get us around, but the tyres! They were tubed in those days and punctures were a common thing. A couple of the tyres on the Singer, although they had plenty of tread, were damaged on the inner walls. This resulted in the loose fabric inside the tyre, chafing on the tube and causing a hole. During our courting days, there was one occasion when we went to the Garrick Theatre at Southport and on leaving, found two flat tyres. I had to put the spare on one wheel and mend a puncture on the other. We always carried puncture repair kits and tools and with this motor they were essential! On another occasion Cath had to hold on to some wires under the dashboard to get us home so I decided it had to go. I advertised it in the local rag and sold it for what I paid for it.

My next purchase was a Triumph Tiger motor cycle. Well, I bought the frame and a large box of bits and pieces which I was assured, was complete when assembled. This turned out to be correct and we had many happy miles together with Cath riding pillion.

Work was the next of my worries! As there was no airport near Wigan and the likelihood of getting a civilian qualification in the aircraft industry was pretty remote, I decided to look for a job in the local garages. There was a garage down the road from Orrell Post at Abbey Lakes, owned by a chap called Jimmy Ind. He was already buying up surplus army vehicles as these were being auctioned off all over the country and there was money to be made from army surplus vehicles as many people had had their vehicles confiscated by the army at the outset of the emergency. In fact, back then, I had delivered a nice little truck to the army depot in Shrivenham, Wiltshire. When handing the truck over, they did their damndest to get me to join the army. This was well before the war had been declared. I thought they can requisition the vehicle but they are not having me! Just give me my rail warrant and I'll be off. I was working at a garage in Darwen at the time so this must have been several months before war was declared.

When I went to see Jimmy Ind he took me on straight away. He had a couple of lads working for him but they had little idea of dealing with customers so I was I/c whilst he was off to the auctions. However, wanting to get married, I could see little future in working in a garage and as for finding a house, just impossible. So, I decided that the only way that I could get a roof over our heads was to join the Lancashire Constabulary. Having a father and brother in the job I was well aware of what it entailed.

Chapter 20

Lancashire Constabulary Training School

It was about this time that my mother became ill. Both Mother and Father went off to London to witness the victory parade and on their return Mother had a visit from her doctor, a family friend, who sent her to Wigan Infirmary for a check up. The big C was diagnosed and she was told that they could operate to remove her leg and hopefully, remove the cancer. The family was devastated. Mother had been fine for years and she was absolutely taken for granted. She would always be there. Food appeared on the table like magic. Cath being with us was a big help. Aunty Till came over to help when she came home after the operation and the family gradually got itself back together.

Cath and I decided that we would get married in May, 1947 in the hope that Mum would be fit to attend.

After completing the Constabulary application forms, getting a medical report and blood test from my doctor, I was summoned to the Ch/Superintendent's Office at Wigan for interview. I must have passed that as I was later required to attend the Police Headquarters at Hutton, Preston to undergo a further medical and an education exam. The result of this was that I was under the required weight of 11 stones. I was told to go home and put some weight on then apply again. I was about four or five pounds underweight. It didn't take me very long as I took to eating cod liver oil and malt and anything else that I could lay my hands on as our food was still rationed. I went down to

Cath's home in Llangrannog for a couple of weeks and her mother fed me very well as there were ways and means in the country. She sacrificed her bacon ration so she was able to keep a pig which lived up at the top of the garden until it was time to turn it into bacon!!

Needless to say, I put on the required weight, reapplied, and was duly called to appear at Stanley Grange, Preston which was the Lancashire Constabulary Training School. This was November, 1946. There were about 6 of us joining at the same time. Fortunately, I had the Triumph with me and so was able to get back to Orrell fairly frequently. We were kitted out with uniform and employed on domestic duties (cleaning) until we were to go to the Northern Training School at Bruche near Warrington, which took place in January 1947.

The winter of 1946/7 was similar to the winter of '40, '41, bitterly cold and loads of snow. We were sleeping in ex-army huts which had been split into individual cubicles. The bedding was similar to my RAF days but the blankets, I'm sure were meant for horses. They weighed a ton and caused me great pain in one of my feet due to having slept with my big toe forced backwards by the weight of the bedding. I ended up limping for a week and my explanation seemed to cause a certain amount of mirth, not only among my colleagues but also among the family.

We were having lectures every day, with a considerable amount of role playing. Most of the evening was spent writing up in long hand, books full of the history of law and the Police Service, together with reams of regulations etc.

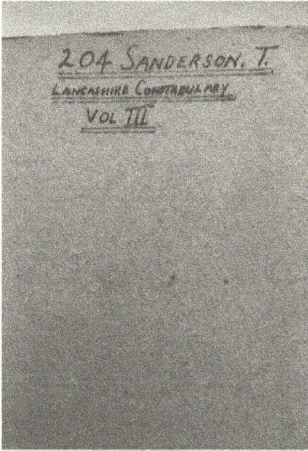

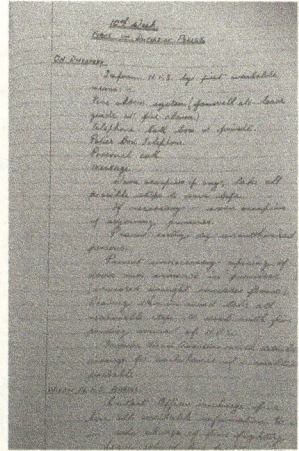

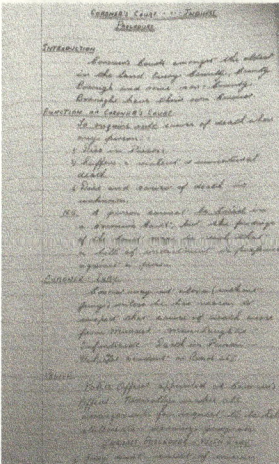

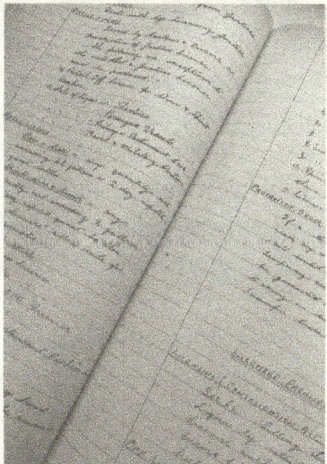

Hand written police info

I don't remember much of the passing out parade apart from the fact that I was in the Gym Display. After the three months at Bruche it was back to Stanley Grange for a couple of weeks local training with the Lancashire Constabulary. My first appearance in front of the public, in uniform, was to attend the Grand National at Aintree. I was given the job of keeping the public from straying onto the course and picking up any jockeys that may have fallen off their horses at the jump known as Valentine's Brook.

After the last race, we assembled at the back of the main stand where we were debriefed and dismissed. As we were paraded in three ranks, there was a room on our right and some feet above our heads, where celebrations were taking place. A number of females decided that it would be jolly good sport to throw their champagne corks at us. We had to stand there while the drunken supporters of steeple chasing were having a good laugh at our expense. Some of the older members on parade suggested that we go up there and arrest the lot but it didn't happen. I have never been to a horse race since unless I was on duty and I never will. I consider it a dishonest enterprise (I can't call it a sport) and cruel too.

There were about six of us who joined together. Names escape me but I remember a guy called Sharples. I'm sure he was epileptic, although no one twigged as far as I know. He would suddenly go quiet and sort of freeze, just for a matter of seconds. He was quite a good artist and snooker player. He would always give me 'three blacks' start and included this in a plaque that he made and presented to me. [*Sadly this plaque has gone missing during the preparation of the book. It was in the form of a shield with a scroll at the bottom bearing the 'latin' motto 'Honistom pro bono Chorley Rodo'. The shield was divided into 4 sections, one with a mop and bucket, one with 3 black snooker balls, one with a Police helmet and one with the motorbike.*] 'Honistom, pro bono Chorley Rodo' referred to my motorcycling from Stanley Grange to Wigan to see Cath, up and down the Chorley Road. The mop and bucket was an indication of our employment at the Grange. I've no idea how I got the nickname 'Honest Tom'. Someone must have recognised an honest person among the many questionable types!!

Another was the son of a Chief Constable of Cheshire I think. He went on to achieve fame in the higher echelons of the job. Another was a guy with red hair. He was the camp jester and had been taken prisoner at Arnhem where they had been parachuted in to save a bridge for the Allied invasion. I think he left the service before completing his 25 years. Another had been a chemist, or so he said. He eventually became a photographic and fingerprint officer at Nelson where I finished my service. Another, name of Roberts, became the Mayor's chauffeur at Nelson. His brother, Caradock, who had also been in the force, became a driving examiner in Blackburn and years later, had the pleasure of failing Cath in the only test that she took. He was very apologetic but said she was so nervous that he couldn't possibly pass her. We had an Austin 1100 automatic then and she got the pedals mixed up on test. She was doing OK until the test but decided that she preferred a chauffeur to dealing with traffic.

Chapter 21

Earlestown

After a couple of weeks of summer duty at Thornton Cleveleys I was posted to Newton le Willows where I was to serve the good citizens of Earlestown for about 12 months. It was here that we met our very good friends, Tom and Dorothy Davies. They lived in a police house in Vista Road and I found digs with a Mr and Mrs Singleton also in Vista Road. I also managed to find a garage for the Triumph quite close by.

When I informed Mrs Singleton that I was about to get married she offered to take us both on. We got a double bed and eventually moved into her spare room. Cath went to St Helens I think, and bought a utility bedroom suite which now still occupies our front bedroom.

The health of my mother was deteriorating. She had had her leg amputated and was paying numerous visits to the hospital with a view to having a prosthesis fitted but the wound was taking a long time to heal causing some delay. May 26th 1947 was approaching and we were keeping our fingers crossed that she would be fit to attend.

Earlestown was a typical Lancashire town. Coal mining and engineering being the main source of employment for its citizens. There were several collieries around and the Vulcan works made steam locomotives, mainly for export and works transport. It was not unusual to see a railway engine on a low loader travelling along the road on its way to the docks at Liverpool.

Pounding the beat in 1947 was a complete contrast to the way policemen operate today. Earlestown had its share of local characters. One I still remember was a window cleaner called Heseltine. My first encounter with him was when I found him in the market square on market day selling a length of thick rope which was about 8/9 yards long, which he had laid out straight across the square, much to the annoyance of the stallholders. He refused to say where he had got it, so I took him in to the Police Station which was about 100 yards away. The local sergeant soon filled me in with the local knowledge which was so necessary in those days. It appears that he was one of the local characters of the town.

He had a son who was also a window cleaner and there was always trouble when they met. Earlestown consisted mainly of two shopping streets. Market Street and I think it was Earle Street. However, they met at right angles to one another. I was out on Market Street on one occasion when I met the local sergeant coming towards me. "Just hang on a minute, Heseltine is approaching the cross roads and his son is coming up Market Street!" Sure enough, the old man was walking down the middle of the road with his head through the middle rungs of his ladder and the bucket also in the ladder in front of him. As the two met, the son pushed the end of the ladder and left his father spinning round in the roadway, shouting all sorts of comments about his son. Fortunately, there was no traffic about. Local characters like that made pounding the beat interesting.

It was at Earlestown that I experienced my first post mortem examination. It was a young 16 year old girl who had been killed in a road accident. As I attended the scene, it was my duty to identify the body to the pathologist who was to carry out the post mortem. Mortuaries were always cold places. I have attended many PM's during 30 years as a Police Officer but that 16 year old girl laying on a mortuary slab taught me more about road safety than all the lectures devised on the subject could ever do.

At Earlestown, we met and became quite friendly with the afore mentioned P.C. Tom Davies and his family. Tom was an ex-Welsh Guardsman and was a few months senior to me. Being Welsh, he had plenty in common with Cath. He was married to Dorothy and they had two young boys, John and Paul. Tom went on to become the Assistant Chief Constable of North Wales Constabulary. As I write this in September, 2008, I believe Tom is still living in Stroud but unfortunately, Dorothy died some years ago. Paul went in for graphic design and John became an antique dealer.

On one occasion, we both attended a sudden death in Earlestown, where the deceased, a man in his seventies, was lying in bed. He had evidently been dead for a couple of days and his wife was still sleeping alongside him. There was a fairly full chamber pot by the bed, and a couple of rounds of toast on a bedside table. His son had visited that day and reported the death. At first, the conditions were such that all did not appear to be a simple, straight forward death, so we turned out the murder squad from force H.Q. at Hutton. When the 'circus' appeared we quietly faded into the background. I'm not sure whether or not Tom attended the P.M. but I certainly didn't. It turned out that the deceased had cancer of the throat and had been unable to eat anything for some considerable time and had literally starved to death. His wife was suffering from dementia and could not assist at all. A sad way to go for all concerned.

It was Tom who had to cover my night duty to enable me to have a couple of days extra leave to get married as there were only certain days that the bus ran to Llangrannog from Aberaeron. He didn't believe me at first. He was from Anglesey and didn't appreciate how remote some parts of Wales were before everyone had motorcars. After promising to reciprocate the favour should he ever need a shift change, all was well and I duly made the trip to Llangrannog. Whether or not I used public transport I cannot remember. However, I made it and so did Cath and happily so did my mother.

Chapter 22

The Wedding

The happy couple

Whilst the war had been over for nearly a year, food and clothing were still rationed and a lot of organisation was required to acquire dockets and coupons to get ourselves kitted out with new suits and the bride's and bridesmaids' dresses etc. How my dear mother-in-law managed to supply all the food I'll never know and was too polite to ask! However, it all came together wonderfully. My parents were able to travel down as were Aunty Till and Grandma Sanderson, Aunty Nelly and Uncle Harry. Brother George was best man and was able to take many of the photographs for us. At that time, his sideline was Wedding Photography. (I think he made more with that than he did in the Police.) Cath's best friend Ray Davies, from Llangrannog and her cousin Barbara were bridesmaids and her cousin Ann was flower girl. It was a lovely day but quite breezy. The reception was held at Cath's home, 'Golygfa'.

The family and guests

And so, on the 26th day of May, in the year of Our Lord, nineteen hundred and forty seven, Cath and I married in Capel-y-Wig, Llangrannog. As I write this in November, 2009 much water has gone under the bridge during those 62 years. Unfortunately, Cath's memory has failed and she has become completely dependant on my memory and the multitude of photograph albums that we have filled over the years. She is unable to operate a computer so I would advise everyone to keep photographs in albums which can be browsed over at leisure. At the moment, they are her lifeline. I am asked questions such as the one she asked me today, "Are you related to me in some way?" It's as if those 60 odd years have been lost for her. Tragic really.

Back to the wedding. George and I stayed the night before the wedding with Cath's Aunty Hetty in Coedmor, Llangrannog. As Mary, George's wife, had just given birth to Chris, she was unable to attend but sent their daughter Janet down with George. My memory fails me when trying to remember who looked after Janet. She was only a baby at the time and all the family attended the wedding.

George and I left the house in a car driven by a stranger to me. Evidently, it is, or was, the custom for the groom to be held to ransom and we were suddenly held up by a guy with a shot gun, who after receiving his gift, discharged his gun into the air and allowed us to proceed.

All went according to plan and we entered the Chapel, walked down the aisle, and as I passed my mother, she grasped my hand, she was delighted to see her second son marry this lovely young girl of whom she thought the world.

Chapter 22(a)

As I sit here to type my memories on Friday, 25th February 2011, tears are rolling down my cheeks as we have just lost my beloved Cath and had her funeral last Monday. She caught a cold around Christmas time. This evidently spread to her lungs and as she could no longer climb the stairs, even with assistance, we brought her bed downstairs. On Friday, 4th February, 2011, Jan was with me when we decided to get the doctor in to examine her. He decided that she should go into hospital right away and called the ambulance. A paramedic arrived almost before he had finished the call, followed by the ambulance and she was taken to Eastbourne General Hospital. The ambulance men put her onto a trolley and as they wheeled her out of the front door, she looked up and said, "Oh. My lovely little house!" This was unusual as she never recognised our house whenever we returned from shopping. I rode in the ambulance with her and Jan followed in her car.

At the hospital, she was eventually admitted to the medical assessment ward and that evening we returned to North Way. The following morning I received a call from the ward telling me that she was in a serious condition and that we could visit any time. I rang Jan and together we went to see her. At this time she could not recognise us. She was wired up to various monitors and wearing an oxygen mask. We stayed with her until the evening then came home for a meal. I couldn't settle and we decided to go back and spend the night with her. She had been moved to another ward and was still unable to recognise us. A doctor informed us that they were unable to get her heart rate down with the drugs they had fed into her drip and that they had done all that they could for her. We stayed with her until about 3am when the staff on the ward said that they would ring us if there was any change in her condition so we came home for a few hours.

Jan stayed with me and we continued to visit and stay with her each day. She didn't recognise us but I'm sure that she knew we were there. On the Sunday, Alice, Cathy and Jan's Tom visited. She was breathing very heavily and was being supplied with oxygen.

When we visited again on the Monday morning, her throat was congested and as the staff were going to clear it and wanted us out of the way, we decided to nip down to Sainsbury's to do a bit of shopping. However, we couldn't settle to that, so returned to the ward where she was back in bed having been made comfortable but still gasping for breath. I took hold of her hand and said, "Not to worry love. Jan and I are here with you." She took another breath and passed away. I was so pleased that we were with her at the end. We had a good, long life together and I have no regrets as I would have hated to have had to leave her first.

Today is the 23 of January, 2012. Only a couple of weeks from the first anniversary of her passing, and I would like to take this opportunity of showing my appreciation for all that our wonderful daughter has done for both of us as we have grown older and more infirm. She dealt with Cath's will in a most efficient manner and has looked after and comforted me like the great person that she is. She has brought up two superb daughters in Alice and Cathy and I am sure that if and when, the time comes they will be as good to her as she has been to us. Thanks Jan! Keep up with the banjo!

I think the story will end right here for the time being as I'm a bit full up as you might say.

28th September 2012

Received the good news yesterday, that Toby proposed to Cathy whilst on holiday in Ibiza and she accepted so there is to be another wedding in the family as Alice and Russell have already decided to marry next year. I think Alice and Russell are arranging it for 8th June. Cathy and Toby are thinking of May 2014.

Chapter 23

1948 Police. Early days

Back to our history!

Our transfer to 33 Ann Street, Denton near Manchester took place in about the Spring of 1948. It was a two up, two down terraced house, with an outside toilet and part of a bedroom partitioned off to make a bathroom. This was to be our daughter's first home as she came along whilst I was still in my probation year. We had a new fireplace installed, and fitted an all night burner. We decorated the living room but couldn't get out of there fast enough. Cockroaches. When on the night shift, I would pop in at refreshment time, do a quick inspection and cremate any that I found.

Whilst doing the decorating, I removed 16 layers of wall paper and a half brick came with it which I duly cemented back in the hole.

My 'boss' at the time, the Ch/Superintendent at Ashton-under-Lyne (now Tameside) decided that he wanted to keep me in his division and found me a place on the traffic group in Ashton-under-Lyne. The first couple of houses I was asked to consider, Cath turned down but the third, 110 Kew Road, Failsworth was quite a nice little semi-detached with a school just a couple of hundred yards away. This we accepted and we moved in before Janice had started to walk.

I had previously applied to join the Traffic Department and had taken a driving test at our H.Q. at Hutton. I was subsequently called to the Driving School to undergo a three week police Advanced Driving Course and became a

The family Kew Road

1st class police advanced driver which is a qualification necessary to operate in the Traffic and Communication Department of the Lancashire Constabulary. Our job was to reduce accidents, enforce the traffic laws, improve driving standards, patrol the major roads and attend all major incidents to establish communications with HQ Information Room. (I.e. the Chief Constable, who used to tell all who may be interested, that he could get a police mobile to any address in Lancashire in twenty minutes.) I answered a call one day for any car in the Whalley area. I replied that I was in the vicinity, and was told to go to Lovely Hall and report back on my arrival. I arrived in about 8 or 9 minutes, reported in and was asked to give a commentary on what I could see. I described what I could see. The state of the garden, weather conditions etc. Received the reply, "Thank you. That will be all." It appears that the Lord Lieutenant of Lancashire whose home was Lovely Hall, was in the Information Room and was getting a demonstration.

There was no such thing as a mobile phone in those days. Lancashire Constabulary were the pioneers of two way radio technology. We had our wireless stations, transmitters and radio workshop where our equipment was built and maintained. This was established before the war and developments were taking place to improve the system. When I joined the department in 1948, we had two way radio in all the traffic cars including the small MGs and progress was taking place to enable the motorcyclists to be included by wiring headphones into the helmets and connecting them to the receiver/transmitter by a magnetic block so that if they parted company with the bike, they wouldn't get their heads pulled off.

MG HTD 166

There were two traffic cars garaged at Failsworth, a Humber Hawk and an MG T/C sports car. Both had 'Police' signs, 'Stop' signs and two way radio fitted. If the Hawk was not being used in the evening and at night, I would use that but mostly I drove and was responsible for the MG. Registered number HTD 166. Most of the maintenance was carried out by the driver and we were allowed 4 hours a week to keep the vehicle clean and polished. Any serious maintenance needed was carried out at either Red Cross Street Police Garage in Preston or The Police Garage attached to Manchester Division at Old Trafford. (This was before the amalgamation with Manchester City.) The other Traffic Patrol Officer at Failsworth was a PC called Jim Morris who was responsible for the Humber. He would have been a 'close fit 'in the MG as he must have weighed 15 or 16 stone.

Headquarters Traffic Patrol Officers, were directly under the control of the H.Q. at Preston (much to the annoyance of the local Chief Superintendent) and as such, could be directed any where at any time. Should a major incident occur, the nearest traffic car would be sent to the scene to maintain communications with H.Q. Information Room at Hutton.

We were often used to patrol areas other than the one in which we were stationed, especially where there were heavy accident rates, when extra cars and motorcycles would be drafted in to cover the 'black spots' during peak times. We were all First Class Advanced drivers and as such could just about quote the Highway Code and Advanced Driving Manual from memory. The system was to stop motorists and issue advice on their driving faults as well as reporting for prosecution. The presence of a Police Car and someone being pulled over and spoken to, had an amazing effect on the rest of the traffic. How times have changed!

It was while I was stationed at Failsworth that our Chief Constable changed. One William Palfrey was appointed.

He had previously been Chief Superintendent at Leigh Division. A first class leader of men with a physique to match. He must have been about 6' 3" or 4", well built and plain spoken. He was also a good P.R. man and loved to put on a show.

When he took over the force he decided to have an 'At Home', one day per year in the summer, when off duty officers and their families could enjoy a day at the H.Q. at Hutton, Preston. In order to provide entertainment, among other things, he decided to have a motor display team perform. He called on the force Motor School to perform a drive similar to that which was performed at The Royal Tournament by The Royal Horse Artillery where teams of horses towing guns and limbers, would perform circles and crossing manoeuvres around the arena. The difference being that we would do it with teams of traffic officers driving MG T/C models. We were given time to practise, most of which was done in a field behind the training school at Stanley Grange and occasionally at the disused airfield at Burscough, Nr. Ormskirk. The year would be about 1952 as far as I remember. I know that we performed the drive at the first 'Preston Guild' after the war. (Preston Guild is a celebration that takes place every 20 years in Preston. There is a saying in Lancashire, when one wants to express a rarity that "it only happens every Preston Guild").

The drive consisted of 18 cars, in teams of 3, driving around a marked out rectangle and when reaching a certain point the leader of each team would turn to the middle and cross the opposing team turning right to go down the outside of the display area and back in again to do tight circles, three abreast, with the team on the inside on full lock and and the rest keeping in tight formation. I believe it was quite spectacular but taking part in it I was unable to see the whole picture. The Chief Constable did the commentary over the Public Address system. It went something like, "You'll notice that the drivers are completing these manoeuvres without the use of their brakes and each one of them will leave here and go to deal with the traffic going to the Blackpool Illuminations" which were taking place at the time. All true apart from the bit about the brakes, as just before lining up in front of the VIP stand at the end, we all flicked the switch which had been wired into our brake lights and they all came on together. (Poetic licence??)

Whether or not there are any photos in existence I know not, but will call on my NARPO members to make a search. The fame spread as Jaguar wanted the team of drivers to go down to Birmingham to do the drive with E Type Jags. But the C.C. vetoed that, despite our disappointment.

And that, I'm afraid, is where my darling Dad's story comes to a rather abrupt end. After Mum died in 2011, his heart went out of it. He died on 22.2.2014, just about 3 years later. In his final few days he told me that the next part of the story was going to be about his "wonderful daughter" finding the MG book on the internet, which amazingly has a photo of the Preston Guild Display Team.

Dad is 4th from the left.

(Right) The officers who took part in the 'Musical Drive' at the Preston Guild at Moor Park, Preston in 1952, photographed here with a couple of the TCs they used.
(Photo: Graham Yeowart, Hutton Driving School)

The Musical Drive Team

These are some diagrams of the manoeuvres. It was all very technical as you can see!

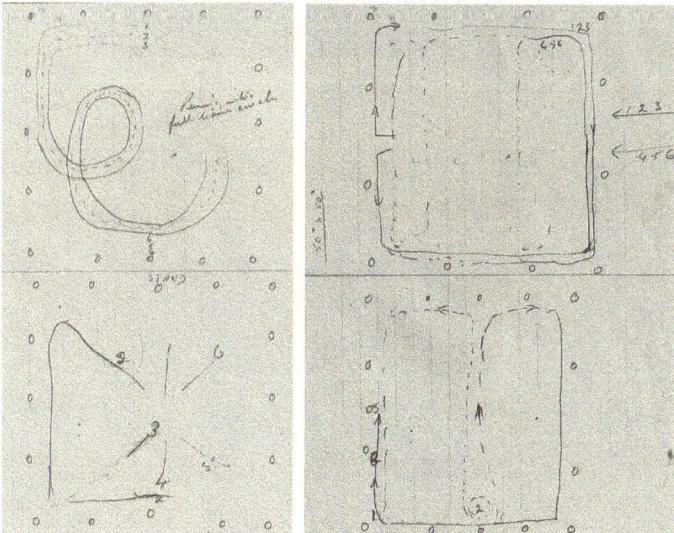

4 Manoeuvre plans

I promised him I'd finish the book.

Chapter 24

Moving round Lancashire

I will try to fill in the main events between 1952 and 2014. Forgive me if I lack his detail and the twinkle in his eye.

Early days

In 1952 we are living in Kew Road, Failsworth the first house I remember.

Dad and me

Mum had gone back to work and I was enrolled at nursery and subsequently at Stansfield Road Infant School. We grew strawberries in the garden which we picked, dipped in the sugar bowl and very much enjoyed.

In 1953 it was, of course, the Queen's Coronation. My trike was festooned in red, white and blue crepe paper.

Red white and blue trike

The carpet was rolled up, the curtains drawn closed and the whole street piled in to watch it on the newly acquired black and white television. It seemed like much more of a spectacle back then in fuzzy grey, than King Charles's Coronation in glorious technicolour. We had tea sitting at a long trestle table at one of the neighbours' houses.

Coronation tea

I played with the cardboard cut outs of the golden coach, soldiers and grey and black horses for years.

Austin 7

Every year in September, we set off to Blackpool Illuminations. I would be in my pyjamas and would fall asleep on the back seat of the Austin 7 to be woken up when we got there. The wonder of the lights and the clanking of the trams only to be topped by a bag of chips at the end.

All our holidays, till I left home, were spent in Llangrannog, a small village on the west coast of Wales, with my dear grandparents, known as Mam and Dada and their golden cocker spaniel Beauty. I adored them all. Life revolved around the beach, the Chapel and the farm where, before her marriage, Mam used to run the farm with her father and brought up her 8 younger siblings after the death of her mother during the birth of the last baby. Dada was a retired Master Mariner in the Merchant Navy.

They had started to build their house in 1923, the year my mother was born. It was a big 3 bedroom villa with a corrugated iron garage on the back which housed Beauty's kennel, the coal hole and an outside sink area which was used for peeling veg and washing clothes by hand in an iron bath with a wooden dolly. I'm guessing there was some arrangement for bathing out there but I never saw it used. The toilet was at the bottom of the garden in the opposite corner to the famous pig and consisted of two buckets under a wooden plank with two holes. In the bedrooms we had chamber pots. I remember when they put the inside toilet and bath in the house and a handbasin in all the bedrooms what luxury! There was no electricity to start with and we used an oil lamp on the big square table. My treat at supper time was extra fried potatoes cooked over the range in the kitchen. Mam would sometimes make a special extra panful for me. Delicious!. Quite often Dada would wipe the floor with us all playing Ludo after supper. I think it must have been a ship's pastime, he was ace. At the front of the house was a verandah where we would sit and watch the world go by. Latterly it was used every day by my great grandfather when he came to live with them towards the end of his life. The big grandfather clock with a loud tick would chime every quarter of an hour and Radio 4 News and the Shipping Forecast would be on the radio every morning.

Happy days with my grandparents in Llangrannog

I love Llangrannog to this day and I'm pleased to say that my daughters and my grandchildren now love it as well.

Mum continued to teach and Dad continued in Lancashire Constabulary Traffic Division until their retirement in 1976. Most of the time Dad would be working shifts, 'Earlies' 6am to 2pm 'Lates' 2pm to 10pm and 'Nights' 10pm to 6am. It would mean being quiet when he was sleeping and many a disrupted Christmas as well as the odd knock on the door from local kids for the 'policeman' to come and sort out 'domestic disputes' between their parents.

It was 'pictures down' and moving house 4 more times. I should explain that 'pictures down' was the announcement that Dad would make when he'd been informed of the next move. They were words we all dreaded. Apparently the reason for this practice was so that policemen would not get too familiar with the local community. I wonder if anybody ever considered the disruption to their children's lives.

The move from Failsworth was to Picton Street, Ashton-under-Lyne, then in 1955 we went to live out in the country at Bescar Lane, Scarisbrick near Southport. Around 1958 the Constabulary built a new garage at Maghull just outside Liverpool. We moved to a new house at Northway, Maghull and Dad spent a few years as a mechanic working regular hours in the Police Garage across the road.

Police Garage Maghull

Then in 1960 it was promotion to Sergeant and back out on traffic patrol and on to our final police house at Lindadale Avenue, Accrington.

Here is an extract from The Lancashire Evening Telegraph Thursday November 1st 1962. They went out with Dad one night on patrol. The headline was "Yellow 91 Heads for Trouble"

"Today we present the men who keep the peace while the world and his wife sleep in safety.

"That's us, Tom." Temporarily, speed is all that matters. The night is black. Roofs are etched with frost. The grey twisting ribbon of a road is swallowed up at a mile a minute ...

Fifty, sixty, seventy! The speedometer creeps up as we tear through the East Lancashire night. The blue roof lamp flashes. Powerful headlamps pierce the gloom. We're in police car Yellow 91 heading for a spot of trouble.

It is 11.30pm. Seconds ago things were "dead quiet" for Sergeant 204 Tom Sanderson, gently sliding the sleek, black car along the outskirts of the rapidly emptying towns. Into his silent patrol crackled the unseen woman's voice on the radio's Yellow channel. *Teddy boys fighting. Penwortham ... Intruders. Lancaster ... Man acting suspiciously. Fleetwood ... Car stolen. Preston.*

The information room at Hutton headquarters spills out in short, dramatic, wireless messages, the late night work for the patrol cars.

Assist PC, disturbance. Accrington ...

"That's us Tom", says Sergeant Eric Hadfield, riding with us. Tom's foot is already firmly down. Fifty, sixty, seventy!" And so the article goes on.

Yellow 91 Heads for Trouble

Nights were sometimes more dramatic

At the end of a long shift

I was now 12 years old and spent my teenage years at Accrington High School for Girls, studying hard and going out with my pals at weekends, dancing to music played by local groups, favourites were The Warriors and The Corner Blues. We ventured to Blackburn, Blackpool or Manchester for the odd Beatles/Bob Dylan concert.

180K Riley1.5 driving lesson

Some of us learnt to drive and attended an advanced driving lecture given by guess who!

Advanced driving lecture for students

Advanced driving lecture given by Sergeant Sanderson
(that's me far left, first row standing)

We were lucky enough to sing and dance our way through Beatlemania and The Swinging Sixties. What fun we had!

When I left school in 1966, I went off to Lancaster College of Art for a year's Foundation Studies. Police Officers were now allowed to buy their own homes provided that they agreed to travel a reasonable distance to work at their own expense and Mum and Dad bought their first house for £2,000 in Pendle Road, Great Harwood.

It was only when I left home and had the first letter from my parents saying how quiet it was without me, that I finally realised what wonderful parents they were. They put up with all my teenage shenanigans and encouraged me to follow my heart, when really, they would have been happier to see me follow my Mum into teaching.

Mum had taught me to cook and sew. Dad had taught me to drive, various DIY skills and marked my card about not believing everything a man tells you! So, off I went to live my life.

Chapter 25

Retirement

Caravanning

When Mum and Dad retired in 1976, they bought a caravan and enjoyed several years touring round "some of this island that we had not visited before". Later, parked outside Pendle Road, it served as a Wendy house for my two girls and their Harwood friends.

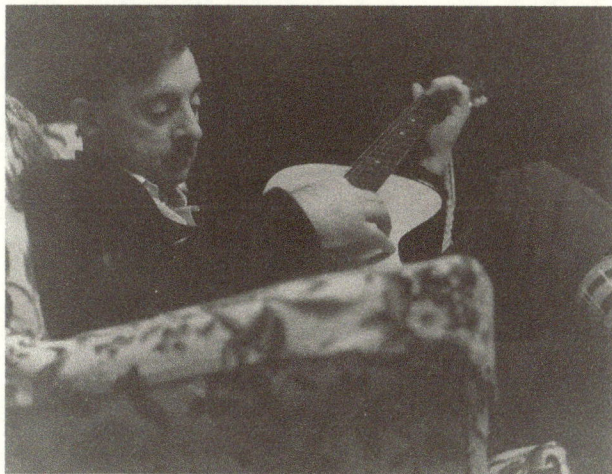

Guitar

Dad taught himself to play guitar and could play a respectable 'Cavatina' amongst other things. I think Mum enjoyed it more than the trumpet! He was playing golf and they were generally having a fine time. They met up with the family whenever there was a wedding or a big birthday.

Doug, Joan, Dad, Tom, George

Doug, Joan, Tom

Mum and Dad stayed in Great Harwood until 1986. My Grandpa Sanderson had married a lady known as "Aunty Connie" who lived next door to us at Bescar Lane. After the death of his 2nd wife "Aunty Evelyn" he had moved in with us, had met Connie and sparked up a romance. They bought a bungalow near Preston and Mum and Dad used to go over to mow the lawn and generally help out. Grandpa died and Connie eventually went into a care home. Mum and Dad used to visit her and look after her affairs. After Connie's death, all family responsibilities up north had been seen to and they started to think about a move south and another set of family responsibilities!

Chapter 26

London and Brighton

In the meantime I had done my 4 years at Art College and got my Dip AD in Graphics from Maidstone College of Art. I got myself a job at Benton and Bowles Advertising Agency in Knightsbridge as a trainee Art Director, got myself a flat share in Brompton Square and all was going well. I met Joe, a musician who played double bass and clarinet. He had been with The Royal Philharmonic Orchestra and was still doing odd dates with them. At the time he was working for a film production company. We fell in love and in 1973 we got married.

Joe and Jan 1.6.73

Joe was quite a character and he and Dad hit it off straight away. There was a mutual respect between them. Dad never missed an opportunity to catch up with him throughout all the years.

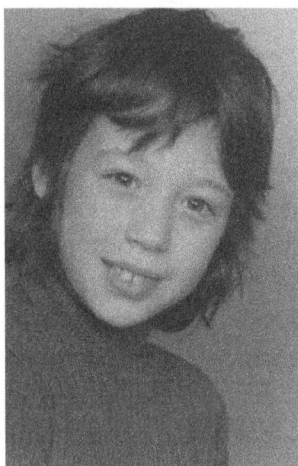 

Mark   Justine

Joe had two children, Mark and Justine, who were a big part of our lives. We would have them to stay every other weekend and often take them to see Joe's parents in Yorkshire and my parents in Lancashire. It must have been on one of these trips when Dad and Justine got locked in the dungeon in Lancaster Castle.

In 1976 Joe and I had bought a big old house in Beverley Road, Chiswick, which we renovated mostly ourselves. Mark came to live with us for a while. I carried on working till I got pregnant with Alice in 1977 and then 6 months after she was born I found myself pregnant again with Cathy. I'm delighted to say that my career in 'Adland' was over and Mum and Dad were delighted to be grandparents.

In 1980 they came down to us in London to celebrate Dad's 60th birthday. His brother George came too and there was much music and fun.

George at the piano on Dad's 60th

George wrote this poem for him in the style of "The Lion and Albert" by Stanley Holloway.

There's a famous seaside place called Blackpool
Wot's noted for fresh air and fun
And in August of nineteen-hought-twenty
The birth of a Sanderson son
Now th'air at' seaside it were sparkling
And Thomas waxed merry and bold
Which were good 'cos when he got to Kearsley
In t' brass band he soon were enrolled.

A good band was Kearsley St Stephens,
They taught him to blow wi' some weft!
If tha' sees a picture in t' band room,
He's thirty-fourth cornet on t' left.

Na many years later the war came
And off he went into the RAF
A'-blowin' a trumpet i' Kroonstad
Or some other far off land gaff.

Then next he went into the Bobbies
But nowt there to blow could he find,
Unless tha' includes breathalizers
Wot's played by the halted and blind!

And so on to t' end of the Bobbies
There's time for thi' muse to tek' wings,
But don't hurt thi' gob on a mouthpiece,
Thi' mun wear out thi' fingers on t' strings!

And tek' up t' guitar like Segovia
Wi' rondos and bourrees and such
There's nowt we can't do if we fancies,
Well leastways there's not very much!

So tek up thi' plectrum and footstool
And join t'other musical fool;
I reckon we've filled t' treble twenty;
I'll give you four in for the bull!

Happy 60th Birthday from George and Mary

Around this time Joe had bought "Makalu", a 50 ft fishing boat which was moored in Brighton Marina so in 1981 we decided to sell up and move down to the south coast. We found a stunning house on Clifton Terrace, Brighton. I was unsure about the move but was convinced by this lovely place, so Mum and Dad brought the caravan down to look after the babies while we got the pictures down and packed up and left London.

Sadly it was not a happy time and Joe and I ended up going our separate ways in 1983. I bought a house in Castle Street Brighton. I got some work from a property developer doing freelance interior design and eventually, when the girls were both at school, I went to work full time doing interior design and graphics at Hubbard Ford, a practice of architects in Hove.

It was during this period that Mum and Dad sold Pendle Road, put their stuff in store and came to stay with us in Brighton while they searched for their 'for ever' home. After much searching they came across a house in North Way, Seaford which was in the process of being built. When it was completed, in December 1986, they sent for their furniture and moved in just before Christmas. They wanted to be about half an hour away from us, so near enough to help out but not quite on the doorstep. It was perfect, we could pop over whenever we wanted without the 7 hour car journey.

Chapter 27

Seaford, a for ever home

At last, they were able to settle and this is where they happily lived out the rest of their days. They were fabulous grandparents just as they had been fabulous parents. They helped me out with the children no end. Dad joined Seaford Head Golf Club and would play 2 or 3 times a week with his FLOGS pals.

BOB TICHENER-KEITH CROSS-ALAN MARTIN-PETER HILL-JOHN EXLEY-MICK HAYHURST-JERRY MILES-GEORGE LYONS
KEITH CRIPPS-NORMAN FOSTER-PETER HORNE-PHIL JACOBSON-ALAN SAYERS-RAY PHILLIPS-TOM SANDERSON-DAVE HOI

Friday Lads Golfing Society

"Me putting on the 10th for a birdie! (missed)"

Winter winner

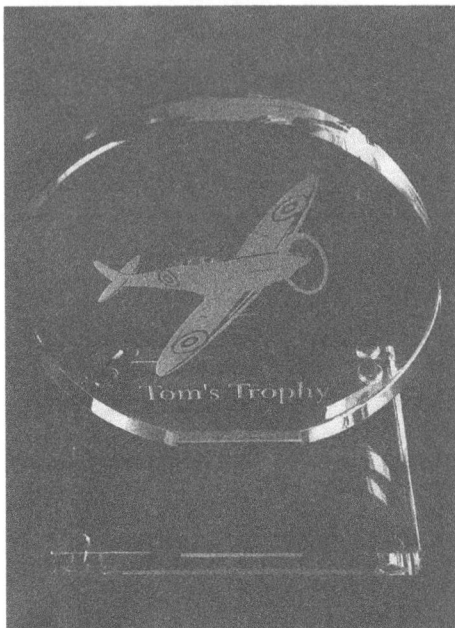

Tom's Trophy

They now have a Trophy named after him and a bench just across the path from his favourite 12th hole.

Dad's bench. Inscription reads 'In loving memory of
Tom Sanderson and his beloved wife Cath. Dearly loved by all'

He got a computer and the internet and dowloaded all the music that he loved. They would visit National Trust gardens and drive around East Sussex exploring.

My 50th birthday picnic at Wakehurst Place

Summer day out

Mum loved to go for "a run to Eastbourne" and always remarked on what a beautiful county they had moved to.

EⁱⁱR

The Lord Chamberlain is
commanded by Her Majesty to invite

....

..........Mr and Mrs Thomas Sanderson...........

to a Garden Party at Buckingham Palace
on Tuesday 15th July 1997 from 4 to 6 pm
as part of the celebrations for the Golden Wedding Anniversary of
The Queen and The Duke of Edinburgh

This card does not admit

Her Majesty's Invite

In 1997 they were invited to the Queen and Duke of Edinburgh's Golden Wedding Garden Party at Buckingham Palace. Both couples were married in 1947 so they shared their Golden Wedding year. There was a coach to take them and bring them home. I think that must have been one of their last big days out.

Off to the Palace

They would both go off to Eastbourne once a week with Jack and Joan, the next door neighbours. Jack and Dad would go swimming and the ladies would do a bit of shopping and they would all meet up for a coffee afterwards.

It was on one of these days out that Mum had her first TIA, fortunately she made it back to the cafe where they had coffee but it scared them both and Dad would never leave her on her own outside after that.

They had sold their caravan when they moved down south and Mum became reluctant to travel anywhere unfamiliar.

By this time I had decided to get a teaching job after all. The girls were hitting their teens and I didn't think it was fair to be relying on Granny and Grandpa to be responsible for them during long summer holidays. So I did a year's PGCE at Brighton Poly and was lucky enough to get a job at Hove Park School teaching Art. I did this for 11 years until I retired in 2003.

In 1995 I met Tom who was also an Art Teacher. We got married in 2006.

Tom and Jan 14.7.2006

The girls were growing up and Alice had gone travelling and then moved into her own place and Cathy had gone to university. Tom and I had bought a camper van and had planned a retirement travelling around Europe. On our first trip to Spain we were away for about 3 months and I read the book 'Atonement'. At the end of the book the writer describes the symptoms of vascular dementia and it dawned on me what was happening to my beautiful mother.

After that we didn't have such long trips and I used to go over to Seaford two or three times a week while Dad went off to play golf. By this time he wouldn't leave Mum on her own. And that's how we organised things for 7ish years until Mum passed away.

During this time we had 2 big celebrations. In 2007 it was their Diamond Wedding, and a big party with all the family, sister Joan and her family, Editha, who was brother Dougie's wife and her family and Janet and Chris who were brother George's son and daughter.

Philip and I are delighted to know that you are celebrating your Diamond Wedding anniversary on 26th May, 2007. We send our congratulations and best wishes to you on such a wonderful occasion and are pleased that you share this special year with us.

Elizabeth R

Mr. and Mrs. Thomas Sanderson

Complete with a message from Her Majesty

Diamond Wedding Cake made by Aunty Joan

The second big do was Dad's 90th in 2010. A similar guest list but this time we had a live Swing Band for dancing. It was brilliant, I got to do a foxtrot with him and he even got Mum up for a few steps. I don't think we've mentioned before but he was a really good dancer.

90th Birthday Party

Needless to say, he missed my mother dreadfully after she'd gone but he kept himself busy. He had all his music on the computer. He would make tiny Spitfire sweetheart brooches out of old coins. We sold some on ebay.

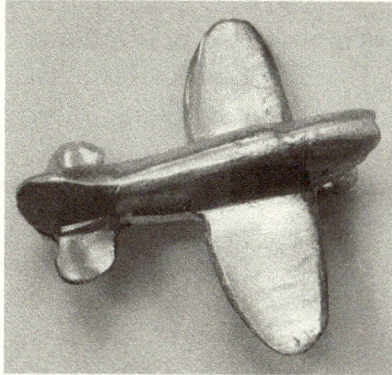

Spitfire sweetheart brooch

He was a great cook and used to bake delicious cakes ... a favourite was Lancashire Lemon Drizzle cake. He'd sometimes share it with the elderly neighbours to "let them know someone was thinking about them." I carried on going over to keep him company and we had some fun learning to play the banjo together.

In his 90's he decided to have a new knee and after a bit of a heart wobble he recovered very well but they put him on Warfarin which he wasn't happy about. We were glad of Mum's wheelchair on occasion.

However, he made it to Alice and Russells' wedding in 2013. At the end of the speeches he picked up the mic and just when we all thought he was going to impart some pearls of wisdom to the happy couple, he announced, "I'd just like to say that, never, in all my 92 years have I seen so many beautiful women in the same place at the same time!" He brought the house down! [See *back cover*] So sad he didn't quite make Cathy and Toby's happy day.

When he found out that, because he'd been born before 1929, he was eligible for a free passport, he decided that he was coming camping with us in the South of France, with my girls and partners and Tom's children, Abbie, Casey and Joel and my friend Annie. It was a wonderful time. The highlight for me was helping him back over the sand after an afternoon in a beach bar drinking cocktails, when a young French lady took his other arm and, quick as a flash, he turned to her and said, 'Merci Madamoiselle'.

Lena Booth would have been proud!

I flew back to England with him and Tom spent a week or so driving back in the camper van. I asked Dad if there was anywhere he wanted to go in the meantime, thinking, maybe swimming at Eastbourne or some such activity. He said "Yes Scotland." So off we went, stopping off to see Joan and the family in Orrell en route. We visited the ancestral graves at Peebles and Roberton and stayed in a little airbnb cottage in Innerleithen.

Camping in the South of France

We went to Kailzie, Torwoodlee and Borthwickbrae where gamekeeper Tom Sanderson (his great great grandfather) had lived and worked. I think it was all a bit too much as he was very weary by then but not too weary for one last adventure.

On the way home, we were about 12 miles into the journey when, after studying the map, he said "Pull in and turn round." He'd found a road, the A708, that he wanted to take from Selkirk to Moffat.

Extract from an article called "My Dream Drive" by Danny Milner on the PistonHeads website "Hills and lochs, just a scattering of remote dwellings and a remarkable sequence of dips, crests and bends; need I say more? the A708 has to rank among one of the most testing stretches of tarmac anywhere in the UK. There are technical challenges aplenty and it's riddled with awkward depressions and cambers that'll quickly separate the men from the boys when it comes to chassis dynamics. Fierce cambers and undulations abound. That means you roll with the plunges, float with the humps and continuously weave in and out of wee burns and clefts as it contours along the side of a valley. After topping out at 338m, the undulations and cambers begin to iron out and the road descends into a long section of sweeping bends. Now you're hugging the shoreline of St Mary's Loch."

I think it might have been a road that they used in Police motorbike training. I told the story in my Eulogy. He enjoyed it a lot more than I did.

He never lost his spirit.

His was a life well lived.

He was the best husband, dad, grandpa and would have been the best great grandpa to Harry, Hetty and Tommy. What a shame they just missed him.

Happily ... 'Life goes on.'

www.ingramcontent.com/pod-product-compliance
Lightning Source LLC
LaVergne TN
LVHW041218080426
835508LV00011B/988